DevOps: Continuous Delivery, Integration, and Deployment with DevOps

Explore the high-in demand core DevOps strategies with powerful DevOps tools such as Ansible, Jenkins, and Chef

Sricharan Vadapalli

BIRMINGHAM - MUMBAI

DevOps: Continuous Delivery, Integration, and Deployment with DevOps

First published: March 2018

Production reference: 1080318

Published by Packt Publishing Ltd.
Livery Place, 35 Livery Street
Birmingham B3 2PB, UK.

ISBN: 978-1-78913-299-1

www.packtpub.com

Credits

This book is a blend of text and quizzes, all packaged up keeping your journey in mind. It includes content from the following Packt product:

- *Hands-on DevOps* by *Sricharan Vadapalli*

Meet Your Expert

We have the best works of the following esteemed author to ensure that your learning journey is smooth:

Sricharan Vadapalli is an Information Technology leader with over 2 decades of experience in leading IT strategy and developing Next Generation IT solutions. Passionate with technology, build practices around DevOps, Big Data, cloud, SAP HANA and EIM (Enterprise Information Management) associated with tech startups, instrumental in devising Go-Market strategy, strong proponent of open source tools adoption, microservices, and containers. Played leadership roles with MNC's such as TCS, Infosys, CSC, Virtusa Polaris, handled fortune client engagements across multiple domains such as BSFI, retail, telecom and manufacturing.

Table of Contents

Preface   v

Lesson 1: Introduction to DevOps   1

DevOps application - business scenarios   3

Business drivers for DevOps adoption to big data   5
Data explosion   5
Cloud computing   6
Big data   7
Data science and machine learning   7
In-memory computing   8

Planning the DevOps strategy   8

Benefits of DevOps   11

Summary   12

Assessments   12

Lesson 2: DevOps Framework   15

DevOps Process   15

DevOps Best Practices   16
DevOps Process   17
Source Code Management   17
Code Review   19
Configuration Management   20
Build Management   21
Artifacts Repository Management   22
Release Management   22
Test Automation   24
Continuous Integration   25

Continuous Delivery   26
Continuous Deployment   27
Infrastructure as Code   27
Routine Automation   28
Key Application Performance Monitoring/Indicators   28

DevOps Frameworks   **29**
DevOps Maturity Life Cycle   29
DevOps Maturity Map   31
DevOps Progression Framework/Readiness Model   32
DevOps Maturity Checklists   32
Agile Framework for DevOps Process Projects   36
Agile Ways of Development   36

Summary   **37**

Assessments   **38**

Lesson 3: DevOps – Continuous Integration and Delivery   **39**

Best Practices for CI/CD   **41**

Jenkins Setup   **44**
Prerequisites to Install Jenkins   46
Standalone Installation   46
Linux System Installation on Ubuntu   51

Git (SCM) Integration with Jenkins   **51**
Integrating GitHub with Jenkins   53

Maven (Build) Tool Integration with Jenkins   **55**

Building Jobs with Jenkins   **58**

Source Code Review – Gerrit   **63**

Installation of Gerrit   **64**

Repository Management   **65**

Testing with Jenkins   **66**
Setting up Unit Testing   67
Automated Test Suite   73

Continuous Delivery- Build Pipeline   **78**

Jenkins Features   **80**
Security in Jenkins   83

Summary   **85**

Assessments   **85**

Lesson 4: DevOps Continuous Deployment   **87**

  Chef   **90**
    Chef Landscape Components   90
      Chef Server   91
      Features of Chef Server   91
      Chef Client on nodes   93
      Ohai   94
      Workstations   95
      Chef Repo   95
    Extended Features of Chef   98
      Habitat   99
      InSpec   99
    Chef Automate Workflow   101
    Compliance   102

  Ansible   **104**
    Prominent Features   105
    Benefits of Ansible   105
    Ansible Terminology, Key Concepts, Workflow, and Usage   106
      CMDB   108
      Playbooks   108
      Modules   110
      Inventory   110
      Plugins   111
      Ansible Tower   112
      Ansible Vault   113
      Ansible Galaxy   114
    Testing Strategies with Ansible   114

  Monitoring   **114**

  Splunk   **116**

  Nagios Monitoring Tool for Infrastructure   **117**
    Nagios – Enterprise Server and Network Monitoring Software   118

  Integrated Dashboards for Network Analysis, Monitoring, and Bandwidth   **119**

  Summary   **119**

  Assessments   **119**

Appendix: Assessment Answers   **121**

Preface

This book is about DevOps which is the most widely used software engineering culture and practice that aims at software development and operation. Continuous integration is a cornerstone technique of DevOps that merges software code updates from developers into a shared central mainline.

So, if you want to implement the strategy of DevOps, you are in the right path.

What's in It for Me?

Maps are vital for your journey, especially when you're holidaying in another continent. When it comes to learning, a roadmap helps you in giving a definitive path for progressing towards the goal. So, here you're presented with a roadmap before you begin your journey.

This book is meticulously designed and developed in order to empower you with all the right and relevant information on DevOps. We've created this Learning Path for you that consists of four lessons:

Lesson 1, Introduction to DevOps, focuses on business trends, drivers, market propellers of evolution, and adoption of DevOps. The key technological concepts are introduced for big data, cloud, data sciences, and in-memory computing. You will also get to know DevOps application scenarios and the benefits of adoption for an organization.

Lesson 2, DevOps Framework, covers source code management, build, repository, release managements, and test automation. Continuous integration, delivery, deployment is also covered along with infrastructure automation for configuration (Infrastructure as Code), application monitoring, and so on.

Lesson 3, DevOps – Continuous Integration and Delivery, describes the CI/CD methodology with open source popular tools such as Git, Maven, Gerrit, Nexus, Selenium, and Jenkins. You will also learn different tools and plugins compatible with Jenkins.

Lesson 4, DevOps Continuous Deployment, shows the popular continuous deployment tools Ansible and Chef; their advanced features such as Habitat, Automate, and Compliance for security. You will go through the core components, architecture, and terminology of Chef, cookbooks knife, Playbooks, and towers. You will also understand how to improve the code quality by using continuous monitoring tools such as Splunk and Nagios.

What Will I Get from This Book?

- Get familiar with life cycle models, maturity states, progression and best practices of DevOps frameworks

- Learn to set up Jenkins and integrate it with Git

- Know how to build jobs and perform testing with Jenkins

- Implement infrastructure automation (Infrastructure as Code) with tools such as Chef and Ansible

- Understand continuous monitoring process with tools such as Splunk and Nagios

- Learn how Splunk improves the code quality

Prerequisites

This book is for engineers, architects, and developers, who wish to learn the core strategies of DevOps. Some of the prerequisites that is required before you begin this book are:

- Prior knowledge on fundamentals of software development life cycle and systems

- Working knowledge of Linux commands

Introduction to DevOps

In the traditional approach to application development and maintenance, multiple stakeholders, departments, groups, and vendors are involved in the overall **software development life cycle (SDLC)**. Most of us are familiar with the stages of application life cycle management: the business requirements are gathered by a business analyst, then developed by the development team (or could have been outsourced), and tested by QA teams (also could have been outsourced) for functionality and fitness for purpose. Performance and stress testing were also performed in applicable scenarios, by appropriate groups with relevant tools. Then the production deployment process, with a checklist and approvals, was managed by the IT teams at the organization, followed by monitoring and support by maintenance teams. And we notice that each stage of the maturity cycle, from functionality development to usability and maintenance, is managed in silos, by independent teams, departments, processes, and tools. This approach is often fragmented by techniques, frameworks, processes, people, and tools impacting the final product in terms of features, cost, schedule, quality, performance, and other administrative overheads such as interfacing and integration between vendors. Also, in this method the maintenance, support costs, and skill needs are often overlooked. However, both from application life cycle and business points of view, maintenance and support activities are key and important to assess, evaluate, and estimate well in advance.

In this lesson, we will cover the following topics:

- Introduction to DevOps
- Business application of DevOps.
- Business drivers/market trends
- DevOps strategy
- Benefits of DevOps

Many technological innovations have taken place to challenge the traditional method of IT management in almost every segment. The technological advances and changes are quite profound, rapid, and often intermingled, encompassing multiple fields such as agile methodology, DevOps, big data, cloud, and so on. A comprehensive and holistic approach will undoubtedly be rewarding and derive maximum value for organizations. Many institutions have already embarked on this journey towards the future, adopting these technologies.

The pre-DevOps software development challenges are reluctant to change in systems; deployments fraught with risk, lack of consistency across environments (**it works on my machine** syndrome), the impact of silos--toss problems across **the wall** such as teams resulting in duplication of effort, skill sets, and in-fighting. To mitigate the mentioned issues and bridge this gap DevOps emerged as a popular choice.

DevOps (Development plus Operations) has recently taken center stage in the SDLC. DevOps offers process frameworks augmented with open source tools to integrate all the phases of the application life cycle, and ensure they function as a cohesive unit. It helps to align and automate the process across the phases of development, testing, deployment, and support. It includes best practices such as code repositories, build automation, continuous deployment, and others.

DevOps adoption for systems including big data systems and projects is a cultural shift compared to traditional development cycles. The purpose of this book is to put forth the concepts and adoption strategy for an organization, covering the technology areas of DevOps, big data, cloud, data science, in-memory technology, and others. Adopting and adhering to DevOps practices will be rewarding for any organization and allow it to improve on its performance and efficiency.

Acceptance of open source tools for each segment of IT functionality, their popularity, and versatility, is increasing day by day, across the world. As a matter of fact, many new tool variants have been introduced to the market for each segment. The open source tools for DevOps are major contributors to the success of DevOps' adoption in the market by institutions, which is discussed in detail in coming sections.

As we can see, across industries DevOps adoption has seen steady growth year on year:

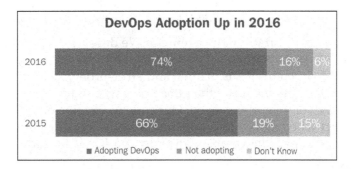

DevOps penetration in enterprises shows a healthy trend, as per the following figure:

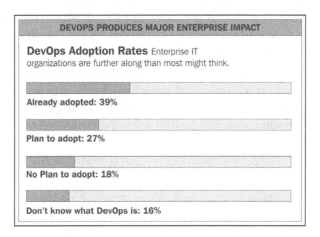

DevOps application - business scenarios

Application of DevOps varies for multiple scenarios, with accrued benefits as listed:

- **Automation of development cycle**: Business needs are met with minimal manual intervention, and a developer can run a build with a choice of open tools through a code repository; the QA team can create a QA system as a replica, and deploy it to production seamlessly and quickly.

- **Single version of truth - source code management**: There are multiple versions of the code, but it is difficult to ascertain the appropriate code for the purpose. We lack a single version of the truth. Code review feedback is through emails and not recorded, leading to confusion and rework.

- **Consistent configuration management**: We develop, test, and build source code on different systems. Validating the platforms and compatibility versions of dependencies is manual and error-prone. It's really challenging to ensure all the systems speak the same language, and have the same versions of the tools, compilers, and so on. Our code works fine on build systems but doesn't when moved to production systems, causing embarrassment regarding business deliverables, and cost overheads to react.

- **Product readiness to markets**: We have a process to develop code, test, and build through defined timelines. There are many manual checks and validations in the process; the integrations between different groups cause our commitments and delivery dates to be unpredictable. We wish to know how close our product is to delivery and its quality periodically, to plan in advance rather than being reactive.

- **Automation of manual processes**: We are following manual processes, which are often error prone, and wish to enhance efficiency by following an automation process wherever applicable. Testing cycle automation, incremental testing, and integrating with the build cycle will expedite product quality, the release cycle, and infrastructure service automation such as creating, starting, stopping, deleting, terminating, and restarting virtual or bare-metal machines.

- **Containers**: Portability of code is the primary challenge. The code works in development and QA environments, but moving to production systems causes multiple challenges such as code not compiling due to dependency issues, build break down, and so on. Building platform agnostic code is a challenge, and maintaining multiple platform versions of development and QA platforms is a huge overhead. Portable container code would alleviate these kinds of issues.

- **On-premise challenges**: We have many on-premise systems. There are multiple challenges, from capacity planning to turnaround time. The Capex and operational expenses are unpredictable. Cloud migration seems to have multiple choices and vendors, so there needs to be an efficient adoption method to ensure results.

Business drivers for DevOps adoption to big data

Factors contributing to wide-scale popularity and adoption of DevOps among big data systems are listed as follows.

Data explosion

Data is the new form of currency--yes you read right, it's as much a valuable asset as oil and gold. In the past decade, many companies realized the potential of data as an invaluable asset to their growth and performance.

Let's understand how data is valuable. For any organization, data could be in many forms such as, for example, customer data, product data, employee data, and so on. Not having the right data on your employees, customers, or products could be devastating. Its basic knowledge and common sense that the correct data is key to running a business effectively. There is hardly any business today that doesn't depend on data-driven decisions; CEOs these days are relying more on data for business decisions than ever before, such as which product is more successful in the market, how much demand exists area-wise, which price is more competitive, and so on.

Data can be generated through multiple sources, internal, external, and even social media. Internal data is the data generated through internal systems and operations, such as in a bank, adding new customers or customer transactions with the bank through multiple channels such as ATM, online payments, purchases, and so on. External sources could be procuring gold exchange rates and foreign exchange rates from RBI. These days, social media data is widely used for marketing and customer feedback on products. Harnessing the data from all avenues and using it intelligently is key for business success.

Going a step further, a few companies even monetize data, for example, Healthcare IQ, Owens & Minor, State Street Global Corporation, Ad Juggler, comScore, Verisk Analytics, Nielsen, and LexisNexis. These organizations buy raw data such as web analytics on online product sales, or online search records for each brand, reprocess the data into an organized format, and sell it to research analysts or organizations looking for competitor intelligence data to reposition their products in markets.

Let's analyze the factors fueling the growth of data and business. Fundamental changes in market and customer behavior have had a significant impact on the data explosion. Some of the key drivers of change are:

- **Customer preference**: Today, customers have many means of interacting with businesses; for example, a bank provides multiple channels such as ATM withdrawals, online banking, mobile banking, card payments, on-premise banking, and so on. The same is true for purchases; these can be in the shop, online, mobile-based, and so on, which organizations have to maintain for business operations. So, these multiple channels contribute to increased data management.

- **Social media**: Data is flooding in from social media such as Facebook, LinkedIn, and Twitter. On the one hand, they are social interaction sites between individuals; on the other hand, companies also rely on social media to socialize their products. The data posted in terabytes/petabytes, in turn, is used by many organizations for data mining too. This is contributing to the huge data explosion.

- **Regulations**: Companies are required to maintain data in proper formats for a stipulated time, as required by regulatory bodies. For example, to combat money laundering, each organization dealing with finance is required to have clear customer records and credentials to share with regulatory authorities over extended periods of time, such as 10 to 15 years.

- **Digital world**: As we move towards the paperless digital world, we keep adding more digital data, such as e-books and ERP applications to automate many tasks and avoid paperwork. These innovations are generating much of the digital data growth as well.

The next generation will be more data intensive, with the Internet of Things and data science at the forefront, driving business and customer priorities.

Cloud computing

Acceptance of cloud platforms as the de facto service line has brought many changes to procuring and managing infrastructure. Provisioning hardware and other types of commodity work on the cloud is also important for improving efficiency, as moving these IT functions to the cloud enhances the efficiency of services, and allows IT departments to shift their focus away from patching operating systems. DevOps with cloud adoption is the most widely implemented popular option. With cloud penetration, addition of infrastructure/servers is just a click away. This, along with credible open source tools, has paved the way for DevOps.

In a fraction of time, build, QA, and pre-prod machines can be added as exact replicas and configurations as required, using open source tools.

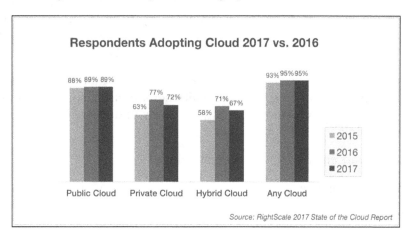

Big data

Big data is the term used to represent multiple dimensions of data such as large volumes, velocity, and variety, and delivering value for the business. Data comes from multiple sources, such as structured, semi-structured, and unstructured data. The data velocity could be a batch mode, real-time from a machine sensor or online server logs, and streaming data in real time. The volumes of data could be terabytes or petabytes, which are typically stored on Hadoop-based storage and other open source platforms. Big data analytics extends to building social media analytics such as market sentiment analysis based on social media data from Twitter, LinkedIn, Facebook, and so on; this data is useful to understand customer sentiment and support marketing and customer service activities.

Data science and machine learning

Data science as a field has many dimensions and applications. We are familiar with science; we understand the features, behavior patterns, and meaningful insights that result in formulating reusable and established formulas. In a similar way, data can also be investigated to understand the behavior patterns and meaningful insights, through engineering and statistical methods. Hence it can be viewed as data + science, or the science of data. Machine learning is a combination of data extraction, **extract, transform, load (ETL)** or **extract, load, transform** (ELT) preparation, and using prediction algorithms to derive meaningful patterns from data to generate business value. These projects have a development life cycle in line with a project or product development. Aligning with DevOps methodologies will provide a valuable benefit for the program evolution.

In-memory computing

Traditional software architecture was formerly based on disks as the primary data storage; then the data moved from disk to main memory and CPU to perform aggregations for business logic. This caused the IO overhead of moving large volumes of data back and forth from disk to memory units.

In-memory technology is based on hardware and software innovations to handle the complete business application data in the main memory itself, so the computations are very fast. To enable in-memory computing, many underlying hardware and software advancements have contributed.

The software advancements include the following:

- Partitioning of data
- No aggregate tables
- Insert the only delta
- Data compression
- Row plus column storage

The hardware advancements include the following:

- Multi-core architecture allows massive parallel scaling
- Multifold compression
- Main memory has scalable capacity
- Fast prefetch unlimited size

Planning the DevOps strategy

A good DevOps strategy, discussed in this book, helps the user gain in-depth and wider understanding of its subject and its application to multiple technologies and interfaces, to an organization provides focus, creates a common (unbiased) view of the current problems, develops the future state, unveils opportunities for growth, and results in better business outputs.

A holistic DevOps strategy, at the most basic level, must answer the following questions:

- What are our business aims and goals?
- How do we plan the roadmap? Where do we begin?
- How should we channel our efforts?

- What are we trying to accomplish?
- What is the schedule for this?
- What is the impact to the business?
- How do our stakeholders see the value?
- What are the benefits and costs of doing it?

A good DevOps strategy for an organization will bring multiple benefits, channel energy to focus on high impact problems, produce clarity to develop the future state, identify growth opportunities, and pave the way for better business outputs.

A DevOps platform strategy will be a unique and extensive program, covering every aspect of the software life cycle, which integrates multiple technologies, platforms, and tools, and posing numerous challenges that need to be handled with skill, precision, and experience.

An organization can consider the introduction of DevOps to cater to specific purposes, such as the following:

- Automating infrastructure and workflow configuration management
- Automating code repositories, builds, testing, and workflows
- Continuous integration and deployment
- Virtualization, containerization, and load balancing
- Big data and social media projects
- Machine-learning projects

There are a wide variety of open source tools to select for adoption in specific segments of DevOps, such as the following:

- **Docker**: A Docker container consists of packaging the application and its dependencies all up in a box. It runs as an isolated process on the host operating system, sharing the kernel with another container. It enjoys resource isolation and allocation benefits like VMs, but is much more portable and efficient.
- **Kubernetes**: Kubernetes is an open source orchestration system for Docker containers. It groups containers into logical units for easy management and discovery, handles scheduling on nodes, and actively manages workloads to ensure their state matches users' declared intentions.

- **Jenkins**: Jenkins is a web-enabled tool used through application or a web server such as Tomcat, for continuous build, deployment, and testing, and is integrated with build tools such as Ant/Maven and the source code repository Git. It also has master and dump slaves.

- **Ansible**: Ansible automates software provisioning, configuration management, and application deployment with agentless, **Secured Shell (SSH)** mode, Playbooks, Towers, and Yum scripts are the mechanisms.

- **Chef and Puppet**: Chef and Puppet are agent-based pull mechanisms for the deployment automation of work units.

- **GitHub**: Git is a popular open source version control system. It's a web-based hosted service for Git repositories. GitHub allows you to host remote Git repositories, and has a wealth of community-based services that make it ideal for open source projects.

There are comprehensive frameworks readily available, such as RedHat Openshift, Microsoft Azure, and AWS container services, with pre-integrated and configured tools to implement.

A few popular open source tools are listed here:

- **Source code management**: Git, GitHub, Subversion, and Bitbucket
- **Build management**: Maven, Ant, Make, and MSBuild
- **Testing tools**: JUnit, Selenium, Cucumber, and QUnit
- **Repository management**: Nexus, Artifactory, and Docker hub
- **Continuous integration**: Jenkins, Bamboo, TeamCity, and Visual Studio
- **Configuration provisioning**: Chef, Puppet, Ansible, and Salt
- **Release management**: Visual Studio, Serena Release, and StackStorm
- **Cloud**: AWS, Azure, OpenShift, and Rackspace
- **Deployment management**: Rapid Deploy, Code Deploy, and Elastic box
- **Collaboration**: Jira, Team Foundation, and Slack
- **BI/Monitoring**: Kibana, Elasticsearch, and Nagios
- **Logging**: Splunk, Logentries, and Logstash
- **Container**: Linux, Docker, Kubernetes, Swam, AWS, and Azure

Benefits of DevOps

Non-adherence to DevOps practices would be challenging for an organization, for the following reasons:

- High deployment effort for each of the development, QA, and production systems
- Complex manual installation procedures are cumbersome and expensive
- Lack of a comprehensive operations manual makes the system difficult to operate
- Insufficient trace or log file details makes troubleshooting incomplete
- Application-specific issues of performance impact not assessed for other applications
- SLA adherence, as required by the business application, would be challenging
- Monitoring servers, filesystems, databases, and applications in isolation will have gaps
- Business application redundancy for failover is expensive in isolation

DevOps adoption and maturity for big data systems will benefit organizations in the following ways:

- DevOps processes can be implemented as standalone or a combination of other processes
- Automation frameworks will improve business efficiency
- DevOps frameworks will help to build resilience into the application's code
- DevOps processes incorporate SLAs for operational requirements
- The operations manual (runbook) is prepared in development to aid operations
- In matured DevOps processes, runbook-driven development is integrated
- In DevOps processes, application-specific monitoring is part of the development process
- DevOps planning considers high availability and disaster recovery technology
- Resilience is built into the application code in-line with technology features
- DevOps full-scripted installation facilitates fully automate deployment
- DevOps operation team and developers are familiar with using logging frameworks

- The non-functional requirements of operability, maintenance, and monitoring get sufficient attention, along with system development specifications
- Continuous integration and continuous delivery eliminates human errors, reduces planned downtime for upgrades, and facilitates productivity improvements

Summary

In this lesson, we have learned about the concepts of DevOps, key market trends, along with business drivers leading to DevOps adoptions across systems like big data, cloud, data sciences, and so on. The business scenarios with ample examples for application of DevOps were presented. DevOps adoption with popular open source tools as detailed in coming lessons will enhance multifold productivity benefits to organizations.

In the next lesson, we will discuss the concepts of DevOps frameworks and best practices.

Assessments

1. Which among the following are software advancements for in-memory computing?

    1. Multi-core architecture allows massive parallel scaling
    2. Main memory has scalable capacity
    3. Partitioning of data
    4. Fast prefetch unlimited size

2. Which among the following are hardware advancements for in-memory computing?

    1. Multifold compression
    2. No aggregate tables
    3. Data compression
    4. Row plus column storage

3. _____consists of packaging the application and its dependencies all up in a box.

    1. Jenkins

    2. Docker

    3. Ansible

    4. Kubernetes

4. Which of the following are tools for source code management?

    1. Splunk

    2. Elastic box

    3. Rackspace

    4. Subversion

5. Which of the following are tools for release management?

    1. StackStorm

    2. Nagios

    3. Logentries

    4. Chef

2
DevOps Framework

In this lesson, we will learn about different DevOps processes, frameworks, and best practices. We will present DevOps process maturity frameworks and progression models with checklist templates for each phase of DevOps. We will also become familiar with agile terminology and methodology and the benefits accrued by an organization by adopting it. In this lesson, we will cover the following topics:

- DevOps process
- DevOps progression frameworks
- DevOps maturity models
- DevOps best practices
- Agile and DevOps

DevOps Process

The DevOps standard processes prescribed across the industry and adopted by organizations are listed here; we will discuss them in detail:

- Source code management
- Source code review
- Configuration management
- Build management
- Repository management

- Release management
- Test automation
- Continuous integration
- Continuous delivery
- Continuous deployment
- Infrastructure as Code
- Application performance monitoring
- Routine automation/continuous improvement
- DevOps frameworks--under DevOps frameworks, we will study the life cycle models, maturity states, progression and best practices frameworks, and also Agile methodology:
    - DevOps project life cycle
    - Maturity states
    - Progression frameworks
    - DevOps practices frameworks
    - Agile methodology

DevOps Best Practices

The adoption of DevOps best practices will help to align people and progress towards organizational goals. DevOps offers multiple process frameworks at every stage of software development. Full-scale implementation of DevOps in an organization requires a cultural shift integrating departments, people, and the process of software life cycles. It enables organizations to move higher on the maturity road map in terms of compliance and process adherence:

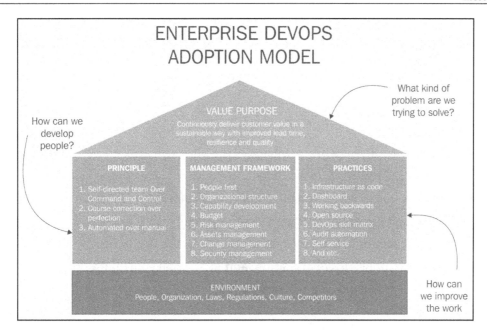

DevOps Process

Now we will look at DevOps standard processes prescribed across the industry and adopted by organizations, discussed in detail.

Source Code Management

Source code management (**SCM**) systems have been in use for decades, offering many functions and benefits. However, integrating them with DevOps processes offers robust integration and automation. A source code management system enables multiple developers to develop code concurrently across multiple development centers spread across diverse geographies. SCM helps in the management of code base and version control at the file level, so developers don't overwrite each other's code, and they have ability to work in parallel on files in their respective branches.

Developers merge their code changes to the main or sub branch which can be tracked, audited, enquired for bug fixes, and rolled back if needed. Branching is an important functionality of SCM, multiple branches of the software are maintained for different major and minor releases, tracking the features and bug fixes across various release versions. SCM enables managing process adherence across environments of development, test and production, facilitating entire software life cycle management from development to support.

The DevOps process framework emphasizes the adoption of SCM for accruing the following benefits for the organization:

- Coordination of services between members of a software development team
- Define a single source of truth for any version, minor or major
- Review changes before implementing
- Track co-authoring, collaboration, and individual contributions
- Audit code changes and rollback facility
- Incremental backup and recovery

SCM tools prevalent in the market are as follows:

- IBM ClearCase
- Perforce
- PVCS
- Team Foundation Server
- Visual Studio Team Services
- Visual SourceSafe

Open source SCM tools are as follows--their popularity is also attributed to DevOps' widespread adoption:

- **Subversion (SVN)**
- **Concurrent Version System (CVS)**
- Git
- SCCS
- Revision control systems
- Bitbucket

Code Review

Code reviews are an important process to improve the quality of software instances before they are integrated into the main stream. They help identify and remove common vulnerabilities such as memory leaks, formatting errors and buffer overflows. Code review or inspection can be both formal and informal. In a formal code review, the process is through multiple methods such as formal meetings, and interactions to review the code line by line. Informal code reviews can be over the shoulder, emails, pair programming where a few authors codevelop, or tool assisted code reviews--these are also called **code walkthroughs**.

A code review process framework benefits the organization as follows:

- Collaboration between software development team members
- Identification and elimination of code defects before integration
- Improvement of code quality
- Quick turnaround of development cycle

Proprietary tools for code review automation:

- Crucible
- Collaborator
- Codacy
- Upsource
- Understand

Open source tools for code review automation:

- Review board
- Phabricator
- Gerrit
- GitLab

Configuration Management

Configuration Management (CM) is the broad subject of governing configuration items at enterprise level, as per **Infrastructure Library (ITIL)**; even the **configuration management database (CMDB)** is part of the CM strategy. Configuration management includes identification, verification, and maintenance of configuration items of both software and hardware, such as patches and versions. In simple terms, it's about managing the configuration of a system and ensuring its fitness for its intended purpose. A configuration management tool will validate the appropriateness of the configurations on the system as per the requirements and its interoperability between systems. A common example is to ensure the code developed on a development system is effectively functional on a QA (test) system and production systems. Any loss of configuration parameters between the systems will be catastrophic for the application's performance.

As per DevOps, the benefits of incorporating configuration management processes and tools for an organization can be summarized as follows:

- Facilitates organizations with impact analysis due to the configuration change
- Allows automated provisioning on different systems such as dev, QA, and prod
- Facilitates audit, account, and verification of the systems
- Reduces redundant work by ensuring consistency
- Effectively manages simultaneous updates
- Avoids configuration related problems of a single version of the truth
- Simplifies coordination between team members of development and operations
- It is helpful in tracking defects and resolving them in time
- Helps in predictive and preventive maintenance

A few popular configuration management tools for infrastructure are as follows:

- BMC Software's Atrium
- Hewlett Packard Enterprise's Universal Configuration Management Database

A few popular software configuration management tools are as follows:

- Chef
- Puppet
- Ansible
- Salt
- Juju

Build Management

Build management is the process of preparing a build environment to assemble all the components of a software application as a finished, workable product, fit for its intended purpose. The source code, the compilers, dependencies with hardware and software components, and so on, are compiled to function as a cohesive unit. Builds are manual, on demand and automatic. On-demand automated builds reinitiate with a script to launch the build and are used in few cases. Scheduled automated builds are the case with continuous integration servers running nightly builds. Triggered automated builds in a continuous integration server are launched just after being committed to a Git repository.

As per DevOps, the benefits of build management processes and tools for an organization can be summarized as follows:

- The vital function of ensuring software is usable
- Ensures reusability and reliability of the software in client environments
- Increases the efficiency and quality of software
- It's also a regulatory requirement

A few build tools that are in use are as follows:

- Ant
- Buildr
- Maven
- Gradle
- Grunt
- MSbuild
- Visual Build
- Make (CMake/QMake)

Artifacts Repository Management

A build Artifacts repository manager is a dedicated server for hosting multiple repositories of binary components (executables) of successful builds. By centralizing the management of diverse binary types, it reduces the complexity of access along with their dependencies.

The benefits are as follows:

- Manage artifact life cycles
- Ensure builds are repeatable and reproducible
- Organized access to build artifacts
- Convenient to share builds across teams and vendors
- Retention policies based on artifacts for audit compliance
- High availability of artifacts with access controls

A few repository tools that are in use are as follows:

- Sonatype Nexus
- JFrog Artifactory
- Apache Archiva
- NuGet
- Docker hub
- Pulp
- Npm

Release Management

Release management is the process of a software life cycle to facilitate a release's movement from development, testing, and deployment to support/maintenance. It interfaces with several other DevOps process areas in the SDLC.

Release management has been an integral part of the development process for decades. However, its inclusion into the DevOps framework makes a complete cycle for automation.

Release management is an iterative cycle initiating by a request for the addition of new features or changes to existing functionality. Once the change is approved, the new version is designed, built, tested, reviewed, and after acceptance, deployed to production. During the support phase, there could be a possibility of enhancement or performance leading to the initiation of a new development cycle.

The benefits of adopting release management are as follows:

- Product life cycle holistic management, tracking and integrating every phase
- Orchestrate all the phase activities--development, version control, build, QA, systems provisioning, production deployment, and support
- Track the status of recent deployments in each of the environments
- Audit history of all activities of work items that are associated with each release
- The automation of release management relies on automating all of its stages
- Teams can author release definitions and automate deployment in repeatable, reliable ways while simultaneously tracking in-flight releases all the way to production
- Fine grain access control for authorized access and approval for change

A few release management tools are:

- Electric Cloud
- Octopus Deploy
- Continuum
- Automic
- Quikbuild
- UrbanCode Release
- CA Service Virtualization (LISA)
- BMC Release Process Management
- Plutora Release
- CA Release Automation
- Serena Release
- MS Visual Studio
- StackStorm
- Rally

Test Automation

Testing manually for every possible scenario is tedious, labor intensive, time consuming and expensive. Test automation, or automatic testing, is for running test cases without manual intervention. Though not all test cases qualify to be automatically run, the majority can be scheduled. Automation is achieved by running the test cases with an automation tool or through the scheduling of automation scripts. Recent test data is used as input and the results are captured for analysis. The goal of test automation is to supplement manual testing by reducing the number of test cases to be run manually--not to replace manual testing all together.

Automation testing is for test cases that are repetitive, monotonous, tedious, and time consuming, that have defined input and boundary conditions. It's not suitable for frequently changing, ad hoc or first time execution test cases. Software automation testing can be based on a few types of frameworks data; keyword, modular, and hybrid.

Testing big data systems encompasses multiple technologies, integrations, frameworks and testing modules such as functional, security, usability, performance, integration testing, and so on.

The benefits of adopting test automation are as follows:

- Improve software quality and responsiveness
- Quick turnaround by substituting manual effort with automation
- Improve the effectiveness of the overall testing life cycle
- Incremental and integration testing for continuous integration and delivery

A few test automation tools are as follows:

- Visual Studio Test Professional
- QTP (UFT)
- SoapUI
- TestDrive
- FitNesse
- Telerik Test Studio
- Selenium
- TestComplete
- Watir
- Robotium

Continuous Integration

Continuous integration is a DevOps best practice wherein developers continuously integrate their code in small logical units to a common shared repository with regularity (for example, once a day). The advantage of such a process is the transparency of the code's quality and fitness for its intended purpose. Otherwise, bulk code integration after the lapse of a fixed time period could expose many defects or integration challenges which could be expensive to resolve.

To achieve continuous integration, there are few prerequisites to be implemented, as follows:

- Using a version repository for source code
- Regular code check in schedule
- Automate testing for the code changes
- Automate the build
- Deploy build in preproduction

The benefits of continuous integration are as follows:

- Availability of latest code as we commit early and often
- Build cycles are faster as build issues are exposed early with check-ins
- Transparency in the build process means better ownership and lesser defects
- Automating the deployment process leads to quicker turnaround

Some continuous integration tools that are available are as follows:

- Jenkins
- TeamCity
- Travis
- Go CD
- Buddy
- Bitbucket
- Chef
- Microsoft Teamcenter
- CruiseControl
- Bamboo
- GitLab CI
- CircleCI
- Codeship

The following figure represents the roles of continuous integration, delivery, and deployment:

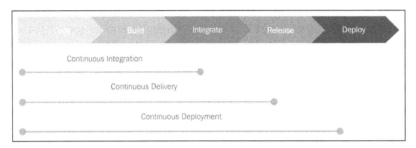

Continuous Delivery

Continuous delivery is the next step of continuous integration in the software development cycle; it enables rapid and reliable development of software and delivery of product with the least amount of manual effort or overhead. In continuous integration, as we have seen, code is developed incorporating reviews, followed by automated building and testing. In continuous delivery, the product is moved to the preproduction (staging) environment in small frequent units to thoroughly test for user acceptance. The focus is on understanding the performance of the features and functionality related issues of the software. This enables issues related to business logic to be found early in the development cycle, ensuring that these issues are addressed before moving ahead to other phases such as deployment to the production environment or the addition of new features. Continuous delivery provides greater reliability and predictability on the usability of the intended features of the product for the developers. With continuous delivery, your software is always ready to release and the final deployment into production is a manual step as per timings based on a business decision.

The benefits of the continuous delivery process are as follows:

- Developed code is continuously delivered
- Code is constantly and regularly reviewed
- High-quality software is deployed rapidly, reliably, and repeatedly
- Maximum automation and minimal manual overhead

The tools that perform continuous integration do the job of continuous delivery as well.

Continuous Deployment

Continuous deployment is the fully matured and complete process cycle of code change, passing through every phase of the software life cycle to be deployed to production environments.

Continuous deployment requires the entire process to be automated--also termed as automated application release--through all stages, such as the packaging of the application, ensuring the dependencies are integrated, deployment testing, and the production of adequate documentation for compliance.

The benefits of continuous deployment and automated application release are as follows:

- Frequent product releases deliver software as fast as possible
- Automated and accelerated product releases with the code change
- Code changes qualify for production both from a technical and quality view point
- The most current version of the product is ready in shippable format
- Deployment modeling reduces errors, resulting in better product quality
- Consolidated access to all tools, process and resource data leads to quicker troubleshooting and time to market
- Effective collaboration between dev, QA, and operation teams leads to higher output and better customer satisfaction
- Facilitates lower audit efforts owing to a centralized view of all phase activities

Infrastructure as Code

Infrastructure as Code (IaC) is a means to perform infrastructure services through the defining of configuration files. In DevOps' scope, IaC is the automation of routine tasks through code, typically as configuration definition files, such as shell scripts, Ansible playbooks, Chef recipes, or Puppet manifests. It's usually a server and client setup with push or pull-based mechanisms, or agentless through **secured shell (SSH)**. Many regular tasks on systems such as create, start, stop, delete, terminate, and restarting virtual or bare-metal machines are performed through software. In traditional on-premise systems, many of the system administrative tasks were manual and person dependent. However, with the explosion of big data with cloud computing, all the regular system activities and tasks are managed like any software code. They are maintained in code repositories, and the latest build updates are tested for deployment.

The advantages of IaC are as follows:

- The use of definition files and code to update system configuration is quick
- The version of all the code and changes is less error prone and has reproducible results
- Thorough testing of the deployment with IaC and test systems
- Smaller regular changes are easy to manage, bigger infrastructure updates are likely to contain errors that are difficult to detect
- Audit tracking and compliance are easy with definition files
- Multiple servers update simultaneously
- System availability is high, with less down time
- Some tools for IaC are as follows:
- Ansible tower
- CFEngine
- Chef
- Puppet
- SaltStack

Routine Automation

Every organization aims to automate routine, repetitive tasks; in fact the survival of most companies and software products is based on the degree to which they automate. ERP systems, data visualization, domain applications, data analytics, and so on; almost all segments are potential areas for automation. A few sections to automate are infrastructure (deployment, patching scalability), applications (development, integration, builds, delivery, and deployment), load balancers, feedback, and defects/errors management.

Key Application Performance Monitoring/Indicators

Performance metrics are part of every tool, product and service. Accordingly, organizations are ever vigilant of the performance metrics monitoring of their applications, products and services. To achieve high-quality output for any product, achieving a high degree of standard in process and metrics is prerequisite. There are many parameters to gauge performance metrics, such as, for example, applications or hardware systems availability or uptime versus downtime and responsiveness, tickets categorization, acknowledgement, resolution time lines, and so on.

DevOps is all about measuring the metrics and feedback, with continuous improvement processes.

Several tools are available for application monitoring for various needs; we will cover the most appropriate and applicable tools in the context of the DevOps framework in further sections of this lesson.

DevOps Frameworks

Under DevOps frameworks we will study the life cycle models, maturity states, progression and best practices frameworks, as well as agile methodology.

Accomplishing DevOps maturity is a gradual progression to being well structured and planned, as stated in the following stages:

DevOps Maturity Life Cycle

DevOps project phases are on lines of the software development life cycle as described here. We will dwell on each phase in detail:

- **Discovery and requirements phase**: The DevOps discovery phase is a highly interactive project phase for gathering inputs and feedback on the current state of process, frameworks and tools from key stakeholders. Templates and checklists are used to capture the inputs. The timeline for the phase depends on the availability of key stakeholders, the existence of requisite documents, and the complexity of the processes to explore. Discovery phase deliverables are as follows:
    - ° Templates detailing the current state of process, tools, frameworks
    - ° Signoff from key stakeholders on the details collated
    - ° Existing best practices and DevOps methods
    - ° Existing challenges, constraints as applicable
    - ° Reusable tools, process, artifacts

- **Design print phase**: The design phase is also the architecture phase; it's about producing a blueprint of the target state to accomplish. It's an iterative process of weighing alternatives for tools, and processes arriving at agreement by key stakeholders. The timeline and cost will be base lined and revisited and revised regularly based on new learnings from the project as we move forward towards the target state. The timeline for this phase depends on how acceptable the processes, tools, and budgets are to the key stakeholders. Design phase deliverables are as follows:

    - Target state is agreed upon
    - Baseline of DevOps process to be adopted
    - Baseline of most viable tools to be implemented
    - Baseline agreed timelines and cost

- **Development phase**: Artifacts base lined from the blueprint phase will be inputs for the development phase; the agreed upon process changes, tools to be implemented, frameworks to be adopted, and so on. A detailed project plan covering deliverables, schedules, dependencies, constraints, resource leveling, and so on will be quite handy. Agile scrum methodology will be the framework to implement the DevOps, which will be discussed in detail. The timeline for the development phase will be as per the project plan base lined initially, and revised regularly with the progress of milestones that have been accomplished. Development phase deliverables are as follows:

    - Initial project plan base lined and signoff
    - Incorporating regular feedback till project completion
    - Allocation of resources for each stage
    - Including new skills, methods, process, and tools
    - Work arounds for project risks, constraints, and so on
    - Deliverables as agreed in the project plan

- **Deployment phase**: The DevOps deployment phase is in accordance with the best practices outlined in the DevOps process framework detailed above. It depends on whether the deployment is a process, an application tool, or for infrastructure. The timeline will be evaluated as per experience gained in the development phase. Deployment phase deliverables are as follows:

    - Deployment guide--cutover plan to production
    - Deployment checklist
    - Signoff from key stakeholders
    - Rollback plan
    - Capacity planning

- **Monitoring phase**: Monitors the key performance factors for each phase's performance of development, build, integration and deployment over time duration. It's followed by tracking the defects, bug fixes, user tickets and plans for continuous improvement. Monitoring phase timelines are as per organization need and performance benchmarks. Monitoring phase deliverables are as follows:

  ° Operations manual
  ° Feedback forms and checklists
  ° User guide, support manual
  ° Process flow manual
  ° Performance benchmark

DevOps Maturity Map

DevOps adoption is a value-added journey for an organization. It's not something achieved overnight quickly, but matured step by step over a period of time with manifested results. Like any Capability Maturity Model (CMMI) or Process Maturity Models, the critical success factors are to be defined for the program's performance objectives. The initial maturity state of key evaluation parameters is agreed upon by key stakeholders. Then the target maturity level of the parameter variables to be accomplished will be defined in the project charter, along with detailed procedure, milestones, budgets and constraints as approved by stakeholders.

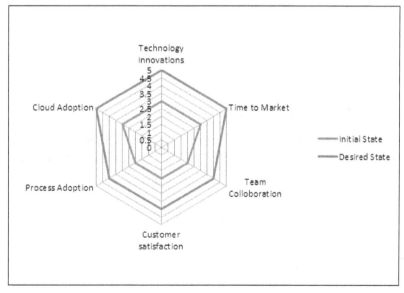

DevOps process maturity framework.

DevOps Progression Framework/Readiness Model

As discussed in the previous model, DevOps adoption is a journey for an organization to higher maturity states. In the following table, different practice areas and maturity levels of DevOps at a broad scale are listed. DevOps maturity levels may vary across teams as per their standards, similarly even a common department or division of the same organization may have significantly more varied and advanced practices than others for the same process flow. Enhancing to achieve the best possible DevOps process workflow throughout the entire enterprise should be the end goal for all teams and departments.

PROCESS	FOUNDATIONAL	REPEATABLE	RELIABLE	OPTIMISED
TECHNOLOGY	Usage by team member	Usage by a Department	Usage by few Department	Enterprise wide Usage
TIME TO MARKET	Ad-hoc Release	Periodic Release	Frequent Release	Continuous Release
COLLABORATION	Team Isolated	Team Communicative	Team Collaborative	Team Unified
CUSTOMER SATISFACTION	Personal feedback	Service level feedback	Department level feedback	Organisation level feedback
PROCESS ADOPTION	Adhoc Process	Inconsistent Process	Shared Process	Aligned Process Corporate wide
CLOUD ADOPTION	Team working with VM's	Department level	Few Departments	Cloud fully embraced

DevOps Maturity Checklists

The process maturity framework, as seen in the preceding sections, is assessed with checklists and discussions. For each of the key focus areas, the detailed findings will indicate the maturity levels.

The findings provide a general estimate of the maturity level and the impact it is causing:

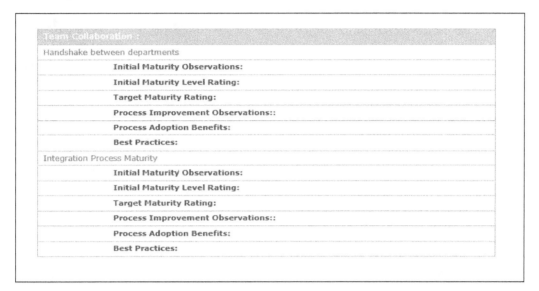

Software Portfolio		
Rework vs. new functionality or value delivery		
	Initial Maturity Observations:	
	Initial Maturity Level Rating:	
	Target Maturity Rating:	
	Process Improvement Observations::	
	Process Adoption Benefits:	
	Best Practices:	
Development Portfolio		
Build Process workflow		
	Initial Maturity Observations:	
	Initial Maturity Level Rating:	
	Target Maturity Rating:	
	Process Improvement Observations::	
	Process Adoption Benefits:	
	Best Practices:	
Deployment process Effectiveness		
	Initial Maturity Observations:	
	Initial Maturity Level Rating:	
	Target Maturity Rating:	
	Process Improvement Observations::	
	Process Adoption Benefits:	
	Best Practices:	

Key Metrics Summary		
Code quality		
	Initial Maturity Observations:	
	Initial Maturity Level Rating:	
	Target Maturity Rating:	
	Process Improvement Observations::	
	Process Adoption Benefits:	
	Best Practices:	
Test Cases Automation and Results		
	Initial Maturity Observations:	
	Initial Maturity Level Rating:	
	Target Maturity Rating:	
	Process Improvement Observations::	
	Process Adoption Benefits:	
	Best Practices:	
Applications Monitoring- KPI's		
	Initial Maturity Observations:	
	Initial Maturity Level Rating:	
	Target Maturity Rating:	
	Process Improvement Observations::	
	Process Adoption Benefits:	
	Best Practices:	

Production Framework :	
Identification of defects	
	Initial Maturity Observations:
	Initial Maturity Level Rating:
	Target Maturity Rating:
	Process Improvement Observations::
	Process Adoption Benefits:
	Best Practices:
Responsiveness/Performance	
	Initial Maturity Observations:
	Initial Maturity Level Rating:
	Target Maturity Rating:
	Process Improvement Observations::
	Process Adoption Benefits:
	Best Practices:
Scalability of systems Architecture	
	Initial Maturity Observations:
	Initial Maturity Level Rating:
	Target Maturity Rating:
	Process Improvement Observations::
	Process Adoption Benefits:
	Best Practices:

Cloud Technology Adoption Progress:
Initial Maturity Observations:
Initial Maturity Level Rating:
Target Maturity Rating:
Process Improvement Observations::
Process Adoption Benefits:
Best Practices:

Agile Framework for DevOps Process Projects

DevOps projects are typically Agile-framework based, for the effective and quick turnaround of the development and implementation process cycle.

Agile software development-based projects have become widely accepted and adopted across the industry. The traditional waterfall model is outdated and unable to keep up with the advantages offered by agile methodology.

Agile methodology owes its success to its core objectives such as:

- Individuals and interactions are valued over process and tools
- Working software is valued over comprehensive documentation
- Customer collaboration is valued over contract negotiation
- Change adoption agility is valued over project plan adherence

Agile Ways of Development

Scrum is the agile development methodology, focused on features development, from a team comprising of roles such as the following:

- The scrum master is responsible for team setup, conducting sprint meetings, and removing development obstacles
- The product owner creates and prioritizes product backlog, and is responsible for the delivery of the functionality at each sprint iteration cycle
- The scrum team manages and organizes the work to complete in the sprint cycle
- The product backlog is the list of features and requirements of functionality to be developed

The Agile method of development is an incremental and iterative approach for developing user stories, software features or functionality. Customers can see the product features early and make necessary changes, if needed. The development cycle is broken into sprint cycles of two to four weeks, to accomplish units of work. The idea is that smaller cycles can be developed and managed quickly with a team of developers and testers together. The structure and documentation are not important but a working feature of the code is considered valuable. The development process is iteratively accomplished in successive sprint cycles. Bugs identified are fixed at the earliest sprint with successful testing. Regression testing is performed when new functions or logic are developed. User acceptance tests are performed after the sprint cycle to flag the product for release:

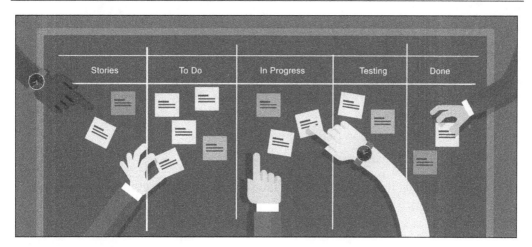

The benefits of adopting the best practices of agile software development are as follows:

- Working software makes the customer satisfied, as he can view the features
- Customers can add change requests at any phase of development
- Quick and continuous delivery of software in weeks
- Projects are built around motivated individuals, who should be trusted
- Sprint teams are highly skilled and efficient in delivery
- Since developers and testers codevelop, bugs are solved within sprint
- The communication mode is effective so quality of product delivered is higher
- Continuous attention to technical excellence leads to good design
- Self-organizing teams focus on optimal architectures, requirements, and designs
- The team is lean and effective, so productivity is maximized

Summary

In this lesson, we understood the application of DevOps processes, frameworks, best practices, and DevOps process maturity frameworks and progression models with checklist templates. We also looked into agile terminology and methodology.

In this next lesson, we will learn about implementing DevOps core process.

Assessments

1. Which among the following DevOps processes offers robust integration and automation?

    1. Source code management

    2. Code review

    3. Configuration management

    4. Build management

2. Which of the following are proprietary tools for code review automation?

    1. Git

    2. SCCS

    3. Crucible

    4. SVN

3. Which among the following are benefits of artifacts repository management?

    1. Ensures reusability and reliability of the software in client environments

    2. Ensure builds are repeatable and reproducible

    3. Track the status of recent deployments in each of the environments

    4. Audit history of all activities of work items that are associated with each release

4. Which of the following is a deliverable of the discovery phase in DevOps maturity life cycle?

    1. Baseline of most viable tools to be implemented

    2. Baseline agreed timelines and cost

    3. Reusable tools, process, and artifacts

    4. Baseline of DevOps process to be adopted

5. The _____ is responsible for team setup, conducting sprint meetings, and removing development obstacles.

    1. Scrum master

    2. Product owner

    3. Customer

    4. Scrum team

3
DevOps – Continuous Integration and Delivery

In this lesson, we will learn about implementing DevOps core process such as source code repository, code review, artifacts repository, continuous testing, continuous development, and continuous integration. We will focus on few popular tools such as Git, Jenkins, Maven, Gerrit, Nexus, Selenium, and so on.

- **Continuous integration (CI)**
- **Continuous delivery (CD)**
- Jenkins tool setup
- Configuration management-Jenkins
- Source code management – Git
- Build management – Maven
- Source code review – Gerrit
- Repository management – Nexus
- Test Automation – Selenium
- Continuous deployment – Pipelines
- Jenkins client setup
- Jenkins security
- Jenkins metrics

Continuous integration and continuous delivery are popular and valuable processes to ensure high-quality and timely software delivery. Continuous integration is the integrated software development process where multiple developers adhere to the agile methodology and adapt it to best practices like the following:

- Ensure all development code is subject to a version control system
- An adequate code review process is incorporated
- Changes to code are integrated, tested, and built quickly
- Build process is integrated to run unit tests and automated
- Attend to the build errors immediately, turn around quickly
- Tracking and Metrics of build results and repository management.
- Transparency and a user-friendly build process

Continuous delivery is the process of extending the continuous integration.

- The most current and latest version of the software is readily available
- Changes passing through the testing cycle from the technical and quality standpoint are ready for deployment
- Automate the shipment and deployment process

The continuous integration process is depicted as follows:

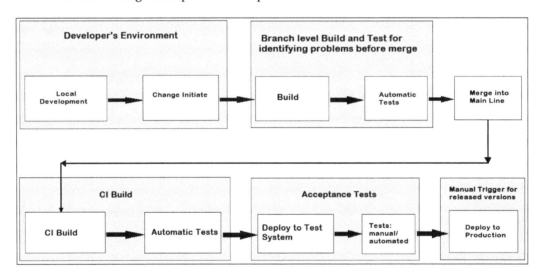

The continuous integration process is detailed following:

- **The developer's environment**: Developers create code changes in a local workspace with an Integrated Development Environment runtime and with build tools physically installed on PC, or a cloud-based (Web IDE). They do unit level testing, data validations, code performance checks, and so on. The code changes done by the developer are pushed to the source code management system.

- The typical continuous integration and deployment cycle is comprises of setting up a CI/CD infrastructure and processes as listed:

  - The source code version and repository management system
  - A process scheduler to initiate the orchestration pipeline
  - A build process to manage code builds and scheduled tests
  - Build nodes for executing the build
  - Testing process on identified test nodes for automated testing
  - Build outcome artifact repository
  - Artefact repository to store build results
  - Scenario and acceptance tests on test nodes
  - Application installation with deploy tool on to runtime systems
  - Acceptance tests for applications deployed on the runtime systems

The quality manager will approve the acceptance tests to agree to deployment test systems.

The delivery manager will approve the application deployment to production.

Best Practices for CI/CD

Let's take a look at the best practices for CI/CD:

- **Using version control**: In collaborative development environments with simultaneous development there will be multiple challenges:

  - A source code management system defines a single source of truth for the code after placing the code under a version control system. The source code will be reproducible by effectively adopting the merge process for mainline development and loop lines for bug fixes and so on in the system. Git is a popular source code management system and GitHub is a cloud variant as a **Software as Service (SaaS)** model:

- **Automate the build**: Standardized automated build procedure will stabilize the build process to produces dependable results. The matured build process must contain the build description and all the dependencies to execute the build with a standardized build tool installation. Jenkins is the most versatile tool for build schedules; it offers a convenient UI and also has plug-ins integrating most popular tools for continuous integration.

- **Tests in the build**: A few tests are to be performed to validate effectiveness and fitness of code beyond just the syntactical correctness of the code as follows:

    ◦ Unit tests operate directly on build results

    ◦ Static code checks on source code prior to developer check-in. Git pre-commit triggers or CI system could be used to set up a gating or non-gating check

    ◦ Scenario tests for new build applications to be installed and started

    ◦ Functional performance of the code

Unit test frameworks are popular across source code technologies like JUnit for Java. Selenium Framework provides graphical user interfaces and browser behavior.

Implementing these tests on the developer's workstation early as part of the build saves time and effort addressing bugs discovered later in the development process.

- **Early and frequent commit of code**: In a distributed development environment with multiple projects, each team or developer intends to integrate their code with the mainline. Also, the feature branches change to be integrated into the main line. It's a best practice to integrate code quickly and early. The time delay increases between new changes and merging with the mainline will increase the risk of product instability, the time taken, and complications as the main-line evolves from the baseline. Hence each developer working with the feature branch should push their code at least once per day. For main branch inactive projects, the high effort for constant rebasing must be evaluated before implementing.

- **Every change to be built**: Developer changes are to be incorporated into the mainline, however, they can potentially destabilize the mainline affecting its integrity for the developers relying on the main line.

Continuous integration addresses this with the best practice of continuous build for any code change committed. Any broken build requires immediate action as a broken build blocks the entire evolution of the mainline and it will be expensive depending on the frequency of commits and such issues. These issues can be minimized by enforcing branch level builds.

Push for review in Gerrit or pull request in GitHub are effective mechanisms to propose changes and check the quality of changes by identifying problems before they're pushed into the mainline, causing rework.

- **Address build errors quickly**: The best practice of building at the branch level for each change will put the onus on the respective developers to fix their code build issues immediately rather than propagate it to the main branch. This forms a continuous cycle of Change-Commit-Build-Fix at each respective branch level.

- **Build fast**: The quick turnaround of builds, results, and tests by automatic processes should be vital inputs for the developer workflow; a short wait time will be good for the performance of the continuous integration process on overall cycle efficiency.

This is a balancing act between integrating new changes securely to the main branch and simultaneously building, validating, and scenario testing. At times, there could be conflicting objectives so trade-offs need to be achieved to find a compromise between different levels of acceptance criteria, considering the quality of the mainline is most important. Criteria include syntactical correctness, unit tests, and fast-running scenario tests for changes incorporated.

- **Pre-production run**: Multiple setups and environments at various stages of the production pipeline cause errors. This would apply to developer environments, branch level build configurations, and central main build environments. Hence the machines where scenario tests are performed should be similar and have a comparable configuration to the main production systems.

Manual adherence to an identical configuration is a herculean task; this is where DevOps value addition and core value proposition and treat the infrastructure setup and configuration similar to writing code. All the software and configuration for the machine are defined as source files which enable you to recreate identical systems; we will cover them in more detail in *Lesson 4, DevOps Continuous Deployment*.

- The build process is transparent: The build status and records of the last change must be available to ascertain the quality of the build for everyone. Gerrit is a change review tool and can be effectively used to record and track code changes, the build status, and related comments. Jenkins flow plugins offer build team and developers a complete end to end overview of the continuous integration process for source code management tools, the build scheduler, the test landscape, the artifact repository, and others as applicable.

- Automate the deployment: Installation of the application to a runtime system in an automated way is called deployment and there are several ways to accomplish this.

  - ° Automated scenario tests should be part of the acceptance process for changes proposed. These can be triggered by builds to ensure product quality.

  - ° Multiple runtime systems like JEE servers are set up to avoid single-instance bottlenecks of serializing test requests and the ability to run parallel test queries. Using a single system also has associated overheads in recreating the environment with change overhead for every test case, causing a degeneration a performance.

  - ° Docker or container technology to install and start runtime systems on demand in well-defined states, to be removed afterward.

  - ° Automated test cases, since the frequency and time of validations of new comments, is not predictable in most cases, so scheduling daily jobs at a given time is an option to explore, where the build is deployed to a test system and notified after successful deployment.

  - ° The deployment to production is a manual conscious decision satisfying all quality standards and ensure the change is appropriate to be deployed to production. If it can also be automated with confidence, that's the highest accomplishment of automated continuous deployment too.

Continuous delivery means that any change integrated is validated adequately so that it is ready to be deployed to production. It doesn't require every change to be deployed to production automatically.

Jenkins Setup

We will start with Jenkins as it's the core component of the continuous integration process. The Jenkins process workflow is shown as follows:

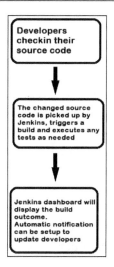

See the Jenkins homepage at: `https://jenkins.io/index.html`, shown as follows:

Prerequisites to Install Jenkins

Jenkins installation and configuration requirements should be planned well as prescribed on the Jenkins homepage based on the following parameters:

- Operating system--Linux versions of Ubuntu/Debian, Red Hat/Fedora/CentOS, openSUSE, FreeBSD, OpenBSD, Gentoo, Windows, macOS X
- JDK version
- Memory
- Disk space
- Java Containers--The Jenkins WAR file can run on any servlet-supported engine such as tomcat or Glassfish application servers.

Jenkins can be installed in different modes as per its utility:

- **Standalone**: Jenkins can run standalone in its own process using its own built-in web server (Jetty) for experimentation and small projects
- **Servlet-based**: It can also run as one servlet framework for development projects
- **Multi-node setup for staging or production**: Distributed client-server setup; the Jenkins advanced installation procedure is recommended

Standalone Installation

A standalone installation as suggested in the name is all by itself on a single machine (as opposed to multiple systems for different tasks):

1. Standalone installation requires JDK to be installed on the system.
2. Download the `Jenkins.war` file.
3. Open the command prompt and, at the location of the `Jenkins.war` file, run the command:

```
C:>Java -jar Jenkins.war
```

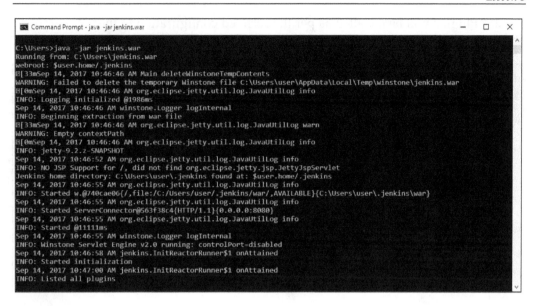

During initialization, a few tasks will run and the following screen will appear during the installation process:

1.   The initial screen page will ask about the plugin options:

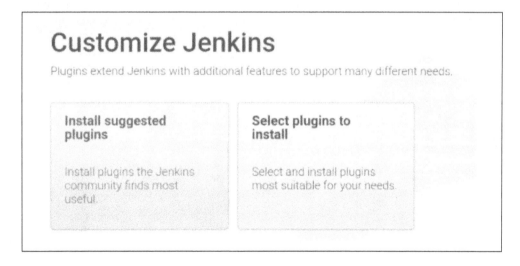

2. Plugins will be installed as per the selected configuration in the preceding option:

3. After successful installation, the following admin credential creation page will pop up:

4. **Accessing Jenkins**: After successful installation, Jenkins can be accessed through a web browser from your local machine as follows:

    ```
    http://localhost:8080
    ```

5. The Jenkins dashboard will open at this link:

6. The **Manage Jenkins** option in the dashboard will provide various options to configure various parameters:

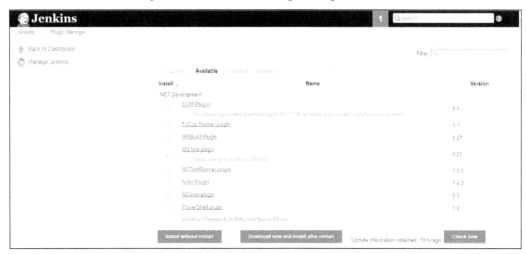
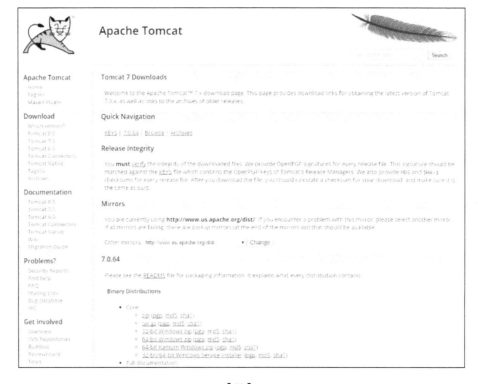

7. The **Manage Plugins** option in the dashboard is an important option with a very wide choice of plugins to integrate with source code systems, authentication systems, various development platforms, and so on.

Installing Jenkins on a Servlet Engine needs the installation of Tomcat or Glassfish.

8. Copy the `Jenkins.war` file it to the web apps folder in the `tomcat` folder.

9. Start the Tomcat server from the Tomcat `bin` directory.

10. `http://localhost:8080/Jenkins` --access Jenkins on Tomcat server.

Linux System Installation on Ubuntu

1. Log into the server and update: `sudo apt-get -y update`.

2. Install Java: `sudo apt-get install -y default-jdk`.

3. Download an Ubuntu version from `Jenkins-ci.org` site using the `wget` command:

   wget http://pkg.jenkins-ci.org/debian-rc/binary/jenkins_2.0_all. deb.

4. Package install `sudo dpkg - i Jenkins.zip`.

5. Dependency resolve by `sudo apt - get -f install`.

6. Access Jenkins on port `http://localhost:8080/Jenkins`.

7. Continue with the steps listed in preceding figure.

8. To initialize Jenkins at startup, add the command `/etc/init.d/jenkins start` in `/etc/rc.local` file.

Git (SCM) Integration with Jenkins

Git is the most popular source code management system and offers extensive benefits such as:

- Version control lets you maintain multiple versions of the code for different purposes

- A code repository is required to keep all project-related code in one place

- Collaboration among users and intervention for debugging purposes

Git can be downloaded from `https://git-scm.com/downloads`:

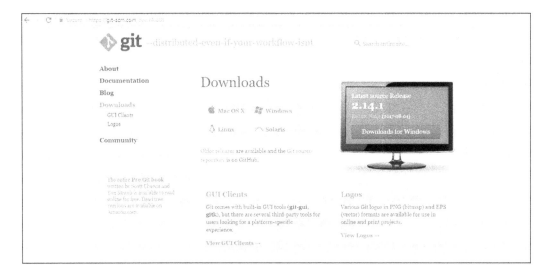

Multiple platforms versions such as Linux, Windows, and so on are available within desktop and web flavors.

There can be multiple types of repositories:

- A public repository created on GitHub can give read access to everyone but write or commit access is given to chosen individuals or groups
- A private repository permits collaborators for participation and is a paid subscription to GitHub
- A local repository is a desktop version without the need for an internet connection
- A remote repository is a web-based repository for extended features like issue management and pull requests

GitHub provides options to synchronize code changes from a single computer or between multiple computers.

Pull changes will sync code changes from a desktop with an online repository and clone options will create a new copy of the repository on the computer.

Performing these tasks enables us to maintain source code on cloud-based SaaS system

1. Create a sign-in account on GitHub.
2. Create a project repository for organizing your project-related code.

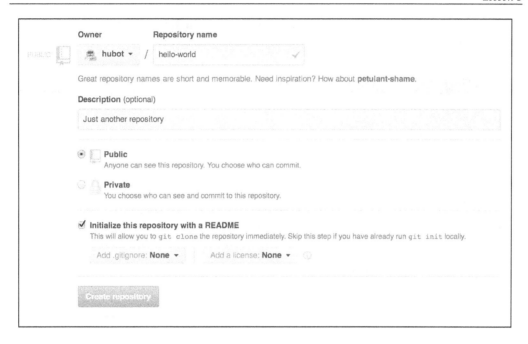

Integrating GitHub with Jenkins

To integrate a GitHub repository with Jenkins, follow these steps:

1. In **Manage Plugins**, search for Git plugin under the filter section and install it.

2. If it's installed by default, we can find it on the **Installed** tab as follows:

3. After Jenkins is restarted, create new item on the Jenkins home page will give the following screen:

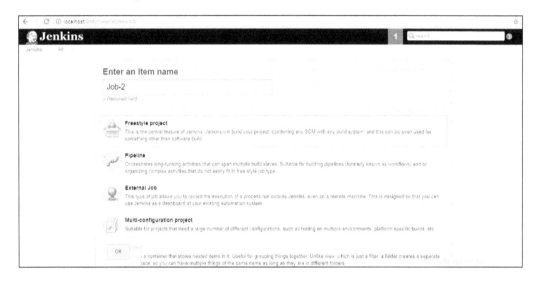

4. Select a job name and the next screen will show Git options as following, under the **Source Code Management** tab. You can add other SCM tools like CVS, subversion, and so on, in a similar manner:

5. Enter the Git repository address of the local machine or a web link in the preceding repository URL placeholder to configure Git with Jenkins.

Maven (Build) Tool Integration with Jenkins

Let's perform the following steps for Maven (build) tool integration with Jenkins:

1. Download Maven from `https://maven.apache.org/download.cgi`; this is the latest version of the binary file:

2. Extract the downloaded Maven file to a folder.

3. Open **Manage Jenkins**:

Select Maven Plugins as follows and install them without the restart option.

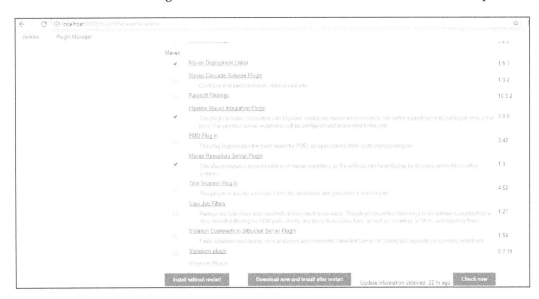

4. Monitor plugin progress as follows:

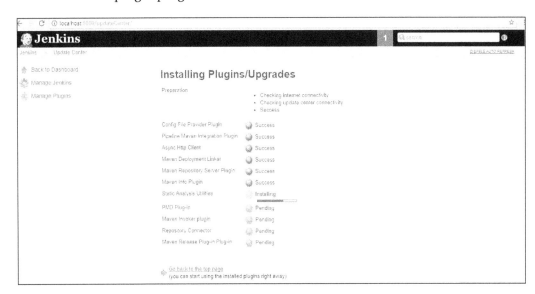

5. Under **Configure** tools, add Maven by giving the repository location:

6. Create a new item job with the Maven project option:

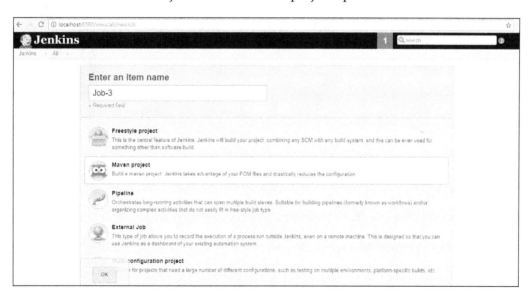

7. The Maven option in build environment is as follows:

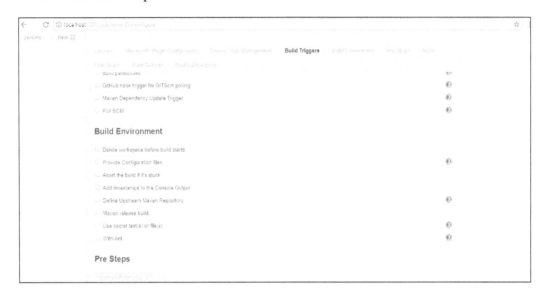

8. The project is created as follows:

Building Jobs with Jenkins

Let's perform the following steps for building jobs with Jenkins:

1. A simple application builds and runs the program:

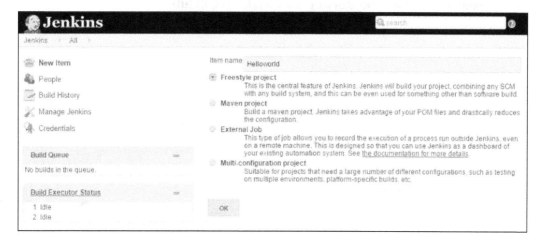

2. The source code repository options as listed as follows:

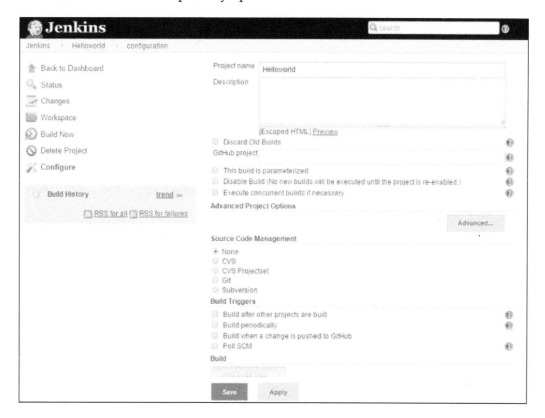

3. We can specify the location of files which need to be built either from a source Git code repository or the URL from GitHub:

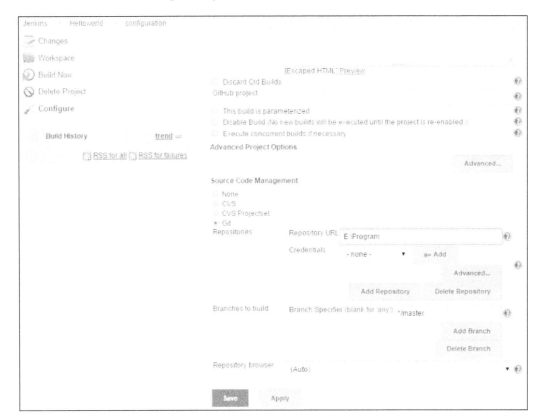

4. Builds can be executed with multiple options, command modes, and Maven and so on:

5. Command-line programs can be executed as follows:

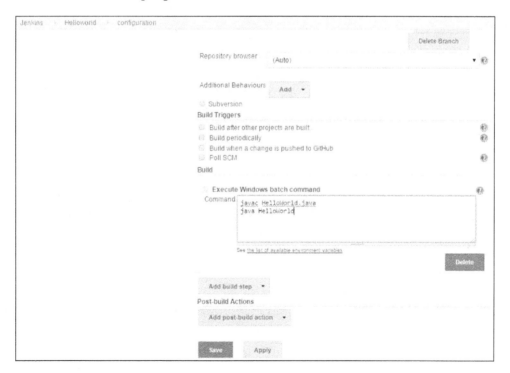

6. After saving, the build option is visible, and history is also available:

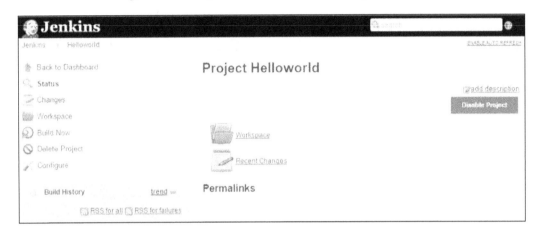

7. Build progress can be seen and repository available as follows:

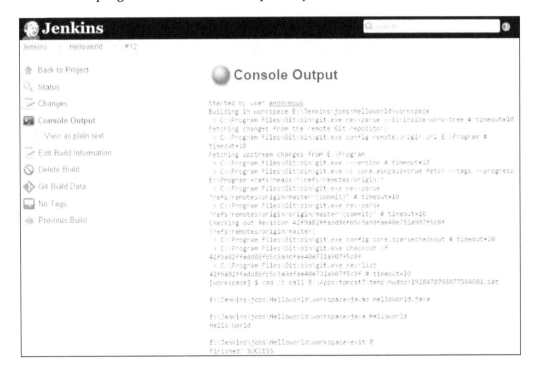

Source Code Review – Gerrit

Code review is an important function in the software development framework. Having a good collaborative tool like Gerrit for a code review process is very appropriate and needed. Gerrit initiates a pull-based workflow to initiate change requests, wherein comments are included even for source code to allow the change to be merged into the code repository through the workflow process. Gerrit maintains a local repository of the mirrored Git project repositories with reference repositories. Gerrit creates another maintenance branch from master branch to track reviews to the code; it creates a change-id identifier for the commit message to keep track of each change in a code review.

Gerrit allows for code change comparisons and a reviewer can give one of five ratings:

- **+2**: Looks good, approved
- **+1**: Looks good, but needs additional approval
- **0**: No comments
- **-1**: Suggest not submit this
- **-2**: Block the submit

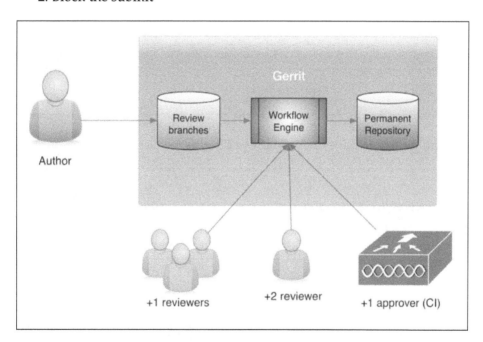

Installation of Gerrit

Let's perform the following steps to install Gerrit:

1. Download Gerrit from `https://www.gerritcodereview.com/`.

2. Follow the installation instructions as per the platform option and access Gerrit on port `8080` as follows to create users and projects:

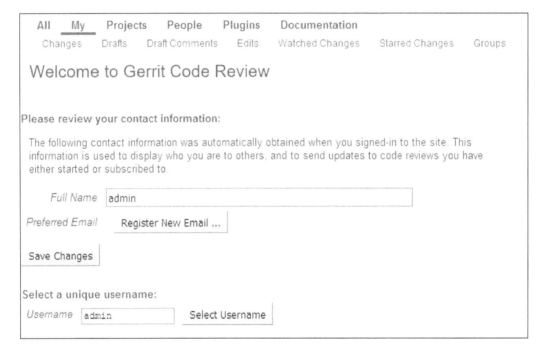

3. Configure in Jenkins under **Manage Plugins** for Gerrit:

Version control tools listed in the *Lesson 2*, *DevOps Framework*, for example Gerrit the web-based code review interface, allow reviewing changes online to push changes from any Git client and then auto-merging them with the master; it can also be configured as a remote Git repository.

Gerrit configuration includes user creation, Secure Shell (SSH) set up to exchange data with a Gerrit server. The configuration file `/etc/gerrit.config` has extensive parameters you need to set as per configuration requirements.

Repository Management

Maintaining multiple build version artifacts is the key feature of repository management and Nexus is a popular repository manager. It can be downloaded from `http://www.sonatype.org/nexus/downloads/`.

After installation, it can be accessed from `http://<nexus host>:8081/nexus`:

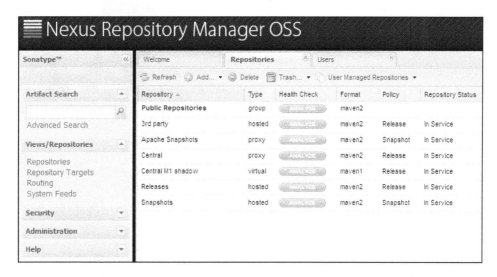

Nexus can be configured with plugins for Jenkins integration:

Testing with Jenkins

Jenkins provides many out-of-the-box functionalities and plugins for testing. The site `https://wiki.jenkins.io/display/JENKINS/xUnit+Plugin` provides the plugins:

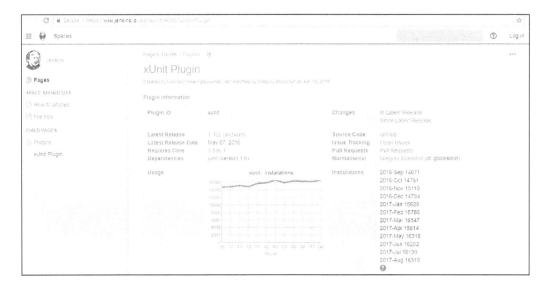

A list of available testing plugins is shown as follows:

- JUnit itself
- AUnit
- MSTest (imported from MSTest Plugin)
- NUnit (imported from NUnit Plugin)
- UnitTest++
- Boost Test Library
- PHPUnit

- Free Pascal Unit
- CppUnit
- MbUnit
- Google test
- EmbUnit
- gtester/glib
- QTestLib

Setting up Unit Testing

Let's perform the following steps to set up unit testing:

1. Pick up the project we have set up:

2. Choose build option:

3. Choose an **Advanced** option:

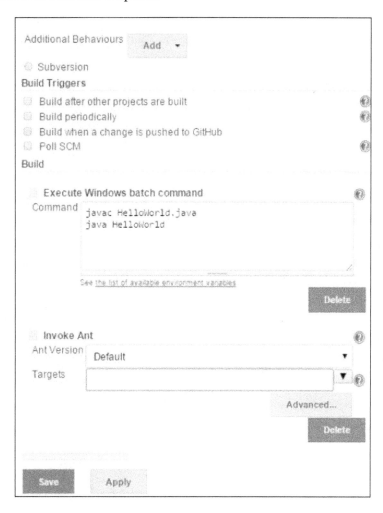

4. Enter the location of `build.xml`:

5. Select the option of post-build option and choose **Publish JUnit test result report**:

6. In the test `reports.xml`, enter the reports created a folder in our project so that Jenkins picks the resulting XML files produced by running of the JUnit test cases:

We can select the build and drill-down to the test results.

Automated Test Suite

Continuous integration is the process of verifying a build to objectively access its readiness for the next level; this is accomplished with automated testing. So, the build artifacts are set to be tested automatically; Selenium is the most popular framework for this.

It can be downloaded from the following site:

1. Under **Jenkins**, **Plugin Manager**, select the Selenium plugin and install, restart to initiate:

2. Configure the `selenium server JAR` file:

3. Configure the project we created to be set for this automated framework:

4. In the build process, add the option, **SeleniumHQ htmlSuite Run**:

5. Selenium IDE will generate Test Suite, the Selenium test is enabled with SuiteFile by launching the Selenium driver:

Continuous Delivery- Build Pipeline

Continuous delivery is the process of building a robust pipeline from software development to deployment.

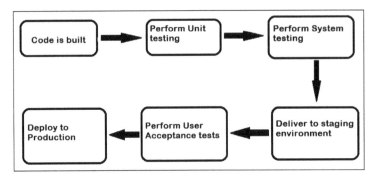

1. Install the Build Pipeline plugin from **Manage Plugins** as follows:

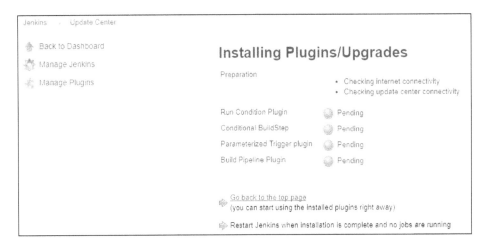

2. To set up the Build Pipeline, Click on the **+** symbol, next to the **All** tab on the dashboard:

3. Select **Build Pipeline View** and choose a name for the pipeline:

4. Select the **Options** and the project created:

5. The delivery pipeline view is created with the status of each stage of the project.

Jenkins Features

- Client-server
- Security
- Reporting

Larger projects need multiple machines to be configured instead of centralized builds on one machine. Also, there are requirements for several different environments for test builds. Slave machines are effective to offload these loads from a master server.

They need a bi-directional communication link from the master through a TCP/IP socket, with only a slave agent instead of the full Jenkins package or compiled binaries.

1. To set up slave/nodes under Jenkins, configure and select the manage nodes option and create a new node:

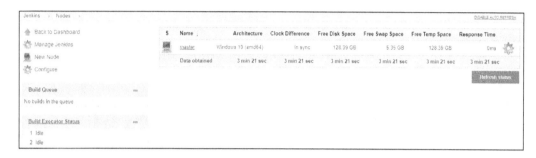

2. Select name and **Dumb Slave** option.

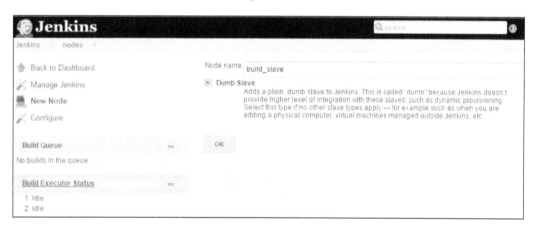

3. The slave node details are to be given, then choose to let Jenkins consider the Windows slave as a Windows service. Details such as name node and login credentials of the machine are required.

4. The slave machine will be available as follows; new jobs can be configured to run on this slave machine.

Security in Jenkins

Users with relevant permissions can be set up with security configuration:

1. Under **Manage Jenkins**, select **Configure Global Security**, and choose to **Enable security** option:

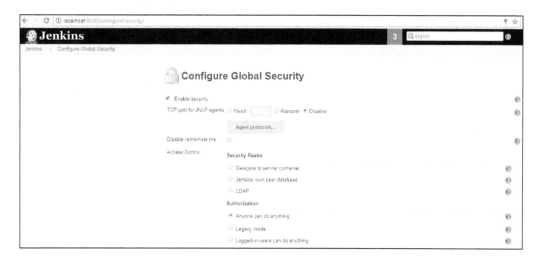

2. Once you save the options, you will be prompted for an admin user.

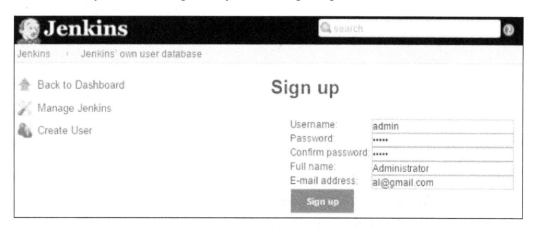

3. Under **Jenkins Manage** setup, choose **Manage Users Options** to create users and then set up authorizations required to execute jobs with matrix based security:

4. The **Reporting Options**, **Metrics Options**, and **Reporting Plugins** can be installed.

5. Many Metrics are available such as the Build History Metrics Plugin:

   ° **Mean Time To Failure (MTTF)**

   ° **Mean Time To Recovery (MTTR)**

   ° Standard deviation of build times

	Last 7 days	0 ms
MITTR	Last 30 days	23 hr
	All Time	23 hr
	Last 7 days	0 ms
MITTF	Last 30 days	2 days 4 hr
	All Time	2 days 4 hr
	Last 7 days	0 ms
Standard Deviation	Last 30 days	52 sec
	All Time	52 sec

6. It can be installed under **Manage Plugins** choosing the **Build History Metrics Plugin**, the above metrics will be reflected on the job page.

7. To see a graphical representation, use Hudson global-build-stats and **Global Build Stats** plugins under **Manage Plugins**. Setting the options, initialize stats, create new chart options, and all the existing builds records will be displayed.

Summary

In this lesson, we learned about processes and tools for implementing continuous development, continuous integration, and continuous deployment with the use of repository management, code reviews, and test automation.

In the next lesson, we will cover the topics of infrastructure configuration management as code for continuous deployment with tools such as Chef, Puppet, and Ansible. We will discuss on continuous monitoring process with tools Splunk and Nagios.

Assessments

1. Continuous delivery is the process of extending the _____.
    1. Continuous deployment
    2. Continuous monitoring
    3. Continuous integration
    4. Continuous delivery

2. State whether the following is True or False: The delivery manager will approve the acceptance tests to agree to deployment test systems.

3. Which among the following are effective mechanisms to propose changes and check the quality of changes by identifying problems before they're pushed into the mainline, causing rework?

   1. Pull for review in Gerrit

   2. Pull request in SVN

   3. Push request in GitHub

   4. Pull request in GitHub

4. Which command is used to install Jenkins?

   1. C:>java Jenkins.war

   2. C:>Java -jar Jenkins.war

   3. C:>Java –jar Jenkins.war

   4. C:>java –jar Jenkins.war

5. Which among the following is the process of building a robust pipeline from software development to deployment?

   1. Continuous monitoring

   2. Continuous deployment

   3. Continuous integration

   4. Continuous delivery

4
DevOps Continuous Deployment

DevOps continuous deployment enables changes to be ported quickly from development to production. Infrastructure and automation play key roles for enabling continuous deployment. In this lesson, we will learn about configuration automation and the implementation of infrastructure automation (Infrastructure as Code) with tools such as Chef and Ansible. We will also discuss the continuous monitoring process with the tools, Splunk and Nagios:

- Continuous deployment
- Chef
    - Components
    - Terminology
    - Architecture

- Ansible
    - Components
    - Terminology
    - Architecture

- Continuous Monitoring
- Splunk
- Nagios

As we have discussed in the previous lessons, the following figure shows the process of continuous integration, continuous deployment, and continuous delivery alignment.

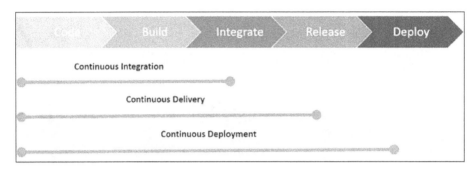

Continuous Integration (CI) is the process of making the development, unit test and build process on a continuous mode as opposed to staggered (step-by-step) methodology. In the CI process, every developer merges their code changes to a central version control system, each commit triggers automated build. So the latest versions are always available in the code repository and also built executable is from latest code.

Continuous Delivery (CD) is a next step to the continuous integration process for software engineering to produce software in short cycles of testing, and releasing software faster and more frequently. The automated testing process ensures that the software can be reliably released at any time.

Continuous deployment is the process to minimize lead time (the elapsed time) between the development of new code and its availability in production for usage. To accomplish this, continuous deployment relies on infrastructure that automates various steps, after each successful code integration meeting the release criteria, leading to deployment, the live application is updated with new code.

Traditionally, a new machine is built by administrators and system engineers from documentation and customized scripts, and so on. Managing Infrastructure through manual procedures such as custom scripts, golden image configurations, and so on, are both time consuming and error-prone. Organizations looking for faster and matured deployments and concepts adopt infrastructure configuration automation, which means managing Infrastructure like a software code for reproducible results, hence it's also termed as **Infrastructure as Code**.

Just like the SDLC process, infrastructure can be managed with similar tools and processes such as version control, continuous integration, code review, and automated testing extended to make configuration changes for infrastructure robust and automated.

The infrastructure code and configuration changes are consistently tested, shared, and promoted across all the environments from development to QA test systems and to- production more easily, rapidly, safely, and reliably with the detailed audit trail of changes. With infrastructure code as a service, the configuration of the new machines to the desired state can be written as a code to set up multiple machines at the same time. This scalable model is more effective by leveraging the elasticity of the cloud. Adopting DevOps to Infrastructure as Code str, and so on goes beyond simple infrastructure automation to extend multiple benefits as below:

- Ensure error-free automation scripts are repeatable

- To be redeployed on multiple servers

- Ability to roll back in case of issues

- Infrastructure code testing standards such as unit testing, functional testing, and integration testing can be effectively enforced

- Since the documented state of the machine is maintained as code and made up-to-date, written documentation is avoided

- Enable collaboration between dev and ops around infrastructure configuration and provisioning, infrastructure code as change management

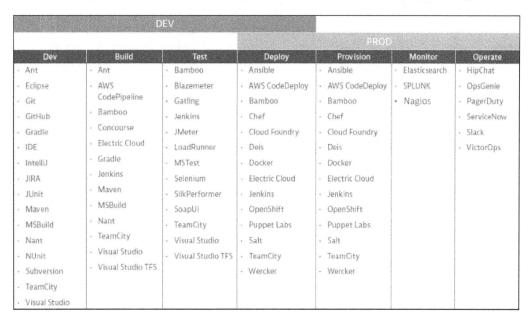

| DEV | | | PROD | | | |
Dev	Build	Test	Deploy	Provision	Monitor	Operate
Ant	Ant	Bamboo	Ansible	Ansible	Elasticsearch	HipChat
Eclipse	AWS CodePipeline	Blazemeter	AWS CodeDeploy	AWS CodeDeploy	SPLUNK	OpsGenie
Git	Bamboo	Gatling	Bamboo	Bamboo	Nagios	PagerDuty
GitHub	Concourse	Jenkins	Chef	Chef		ServiceNow
Gradle	Electric Cloud	JMeter	Cloud Foundry	Cloud Foundry		Slack
IDE	Gradle	LoadRunner	Deis	Deis		VictorOps
IntelliJ	Jenkins	MSTest	Docker	Docker		
JIRA	Maven	Selenium	Electric Cloud	Electric Cloud		
JUnit	MSBuild	SilkPerformer	Jenkins	Jenkins		
Maven	Nant	SoapUI	OpenShift	OpenShift		
MSBuild	TeamCity	TeamCity	Puppet Labs	Puppet Labs		
Nant	Visual Studio	Visual Studio	Salt	Salt		
NUnit	Visual Studio TFS	Visual Studio TFS	TeamCity	TeamCity		
Subversion			Wercker	Wercker		
TeamCity						
Visual Studio						

We will discuss continuous deployment from the perspective of popular tool features and functionality listed in the preceding figure.

Chef

Chef is one of the prominent configuration management and infrastructure automation platforms; it provides a full suite of enterprise capabilities such as workflow, visibility, and compliance. It enables continuous deployments for both infrastructure and applications from development to production. Infrastructure configuration automation as code is written, tested, deployed, and managed by Chef across networks such as the cloud, on-premises, or hybrid environments with comprehensive 24 x 7 support services. Examples are client systems, security patches can be updated from master server by writing configurations as a set of instructions and executed on multiple nodes simultaneously.

The Chef platform as shown in the following figure, supports multiple environments such as Amazon Web Services, Azure, VMware, OpenStack, Google Cloud, and so on. Platforms such as Windows, Linux, VMware, and so on, are available. All the popular continuous integration tools such as Bitbucket, Jenkins, GitHub, CircleCI, and so on, are supported for workflow integration. The runtime environment is available on Kubernetes, Docker, and Swarm.

Chef Landscape Components

The Chef landscape comprising various elements of Chef, including the nodes, the server, and the workstation along with their relationships is shown here. We will discuss each of the components, the terminology, and the role it plays in the ecosystem to enable a Chef client to execute the job assigned. Chef terminology resembles food preparation. Cookbooks are the formula to make food dishes and recipes are ingredients.

The components of Chef are:

- Chef server
- Chef client
- Chef workstation
- Chef repo

Chef Server

The Chef server is the hub for maintaining the configuration data across the network, storing cookbooks, applying policies to nodes, and each registered node detailed metadata managed by the Chef client. Chef server provides configuration details, such as recipes, templates, and file distributions through the Chef client installed on the respective nodes. Accordingly, the Chef clients implement the configuration on their nodes relieving the Chef server of any processing tasks. This model is scalable to consistently apply the configuration throughout the organization.

Features of Chef Server

Web-enabled user interface with management console and search.

- Management console on the chef server is a web-based interface for managing multiple functions such as:
    - Nodes in the network
    - Cookbooks and recipes
    - Roles assigned
    - Data bags--JSON data stores, might include encrypted data
    - Environment details
    - Search facility for indexed data
    - Administrative user accounts and data for chef server access

- Search functionality facilitates querying any types of data indexed on Chef server such as nodes, roles, platforms, environments, data bags, and so on. The Apache Solr search engine is the base search engine and extends all the features such as pattern search with exact, wildcard, range, and fuzzy. A full indexed search can be run with different options within the recipe, command line, management console search feature, and so on.

- Data bags are located in a secure sub-area on the Chef server; they store sensitive data such as passwords, user account data, and other confidential types of data. They can only be accessed by nodes with the authentic SSL certificates validated by the Chef server. A data bag is accessed by the Chef server with its global variables stored in JSON format. It can be searched and accessed by recipe and loaded.

- A policy defines how roles, environments, and cookbook versions are to be implemented in the business and operational requirements, processes, and production workflows:

  ° A role is a way to assign the tasks based on specific functions, patterns, and processes performed in an organization such as power or business user, and so on. Each node, web, or database server consists of unique attributes and a run list is assigned per role. When a node is to perform a task, it compares its attributes list with those required to execute the function. The Chef client ensures the attributes and run lists are up-to-date with those on the server.

  ° Environments reflect organizations real-life requirements such as development, staging, or production systems, each are maintained with a cookbook version.

  ° Cookbooks maintain organization-specific configuration policies. Different cookbook versions are maintained such as source control with associated environments, metadata, run lists for different needs; they are uploaded on to a Chef server and applied by a Chef client while configuring the nodes. A cookbook defines a scenario and everything that is required to support that scenario is contained such as:

  ° Recipes that specify which resources to use and the order as well

  ° Attribute values

  ° File distributions

  ° Templates

  ° Chef extensions such as custom resources and libraries

  ° A run-list contains all the required information for Chef to configure a node to a desired state. It is an ordered list of roles and recipes specified in the exact order to be run to reach its intended state. It's tailored for each node and stored on the Chef server as part of the node object. It is maintained using knife commands or using the Chef management console on the workstation and uploaded to the Chef server.

Chef Client on nodes

Chef clients can be installed on different node types--physical, virtual, cloud, network device, and so on, that are registered with Chef server.

- Types of nodes:
  - ° A physical node is an active device (system or virtual machine) attached to a network on which a Chef client is installed to communicate with a Chef server.

  - ° A cloud-based node is hosted in external cloud environments such as AWS, Microsoft Azure OpenStack, Google Compute Engine, or Rackspace. Knife with plugins provides support for external cloud-based services and creates instances to deploy, configure, and maintain those instances.

  - ° A virtual node is a system that runs like a software implementation without direct physical machine access.

  - ° A network node such as a switch can be configured with Chef and automated for physical and logical Ethernet link properties and VLANs. Examples of network devices are Juniper Networks, Arista, Cisco, and F5.

  - ° Containers are virtual systems running individual configurations sharing the same operating system. Containers are effective at managing distributed and scalable applications and services.

- Chef client:
  - ° The Chef client does the actual configuration. It contacts the Chef server periodically to retrieve the latest cookbooks to update the current state of the node, if required, in accordance with the cookbook instructions. This iterative process is enforced by business policy to ensure the network is in accordance with the envisioned target state.

  - ° The Chef client is the local agent that is installed and runs on every node registered with the Chef server to ensure the node is at the expected state. Chef client does most of the computational effort. It's typically a virtual machine, container instance, or physical server.

- ° Authentication between Chef client with the Chef server happens through RSA public key/pairs for every transaction request. The data stored on the Chef server is shared after authentication of registered nodes. Any unauthorized data access is avoided.

- ° After installation of the chef client, the nodes become compute resources on infrastructure that is managed by Chef for performing the tasks such as:

- ° Registering the node with the Chef server

- ° Authentication services

- ° Creating the node object

- ° Synchronizing cookbooks with Chef server

- ° The required cookbooks, with recipes, attributes, and all other dependencies, are compiled and loaded

- ° Configuring the node as per the requirements

- ° Exception handling and notifications

Ohai

Ohai is a tool run by Chef client to collect system configuration and metrics data with many built-in plugins to determine the system state for use within cookbooks. The metrics collected by Ohai are:

- Operating System
- Kernel
- Host names
- Fully-qualified domain names
- Virtualization
- Cloud service provider metadata
- Network
- Memory
- Disk
- CPU

Attributes that are collected by Ohai are automatically used by the Chef client to ensure that these attributes remain consistent with the definitions on the server.

Workstations

Workstations facilitate users to author, test, and maintain cookbooks and interact with the Chef server and nodes. The Chef development toolkit is also installed and configured on a workstation. The Chef development kit is a package comprising prescribed sets of tools, and includes Chef, the command-line tools, Test Kitchen, ChefSpec, Berkshelf, and a few others. Users use workstations for:

- Developing the cookbooks and test recipes
- Testing the Chef code in different environments
- Version source control synchronized with Chef repo
- Defining and configuring roles and environments and organizational policy
- Enforcing data bags are used for storing the critical data
- Performing a bootstrap operation on nodes

Cookbooks are repositories for files, templates, recipes, attributes, libraries, custom resources, tests, and metadata. Chef client configures each node in the organization through cookbooks and recipes, the fundamental unit of configuration is the cookbook and provides structure to your recipes. Infrastructure state is defined as a file, a template, or a package in policy distribution as per the required scenario.

The programming language for Chef cookbooks is Ruby as a full-fledged programming language with syntax definitions. Recipes are simple patterns for specific configuration items such as packages, files, services, templates, and users with blocks that define properties and values that map to them. Recipes are the fundamental configuration element in a cookbook. A Chef recipe is a file that groups related resources, such as everything needed to configure a web server, database server, or a load balancer. Recipes are stored in cookbooks and can have dependencies on other recipes.

Chef Repo

The Chef repo, as the name suggests, is the repository artifact to author, test, and maintain the cookbooks. The Chef repo is managed like source code, synchronizing with a version control system (such as GitHub, Bitbucket, and so on). The Chef repo directory structure can contain a Chef repo for every cookbook or all of their cookbooks in a single Chef repo.

The `knife` is a command interface to communicate with the Chef server from the workstation to upload the cookbooks. To specify configuration details, the `knife.rb` file is used, `knife` helps to manage:

- Nodes bootstrapping
- Recipes and cookbooks
- Environments, roles, and data bags
- Various cloud environment resources
- Chef client installation to nodes
- Chef server indexed data search features

The package of tools and utilities to work with Chef is called **Chef Development Kit (Chef DK)**. It includes command-line tools interacting with Chef such as `knife` Chef server and Chef clients and with local Chef code repository (`chef-repo`). The components of Chef DK are as follows:

- Chef client
- `Chef` and `knife` command-line tools
- Test Kitchen, Cookstyle, and Foodcritic as testing tools
- Compliance and security requirements with InSpec as executable code
- Cookbooks are authored to upload to Chef server
- To encryption and decryption of data bag items is with Chef-Vault using the public keys for registered nodes
- Cookbooks dependency manager
- Workflow tool Chef
- Unit testing framework Chef Specto tests resources locally
- For style-checking to write clean cookbooks Rubocop-based tool Cookstyle
- Continuous delivery workflow on Chef Automate server also command-line tools to set up and execute
- For static analysis of recipe code Foodcritic is a lint tool
- It is to test cookbooks across platforms, an integration testing framework tool is Test Kitchen
- For rapid cookbook testing and container development `kitchen-dokken` is `test-kitchen` plugin with a driver, transport, and provisioner for using Docker and Chef
- Kitchen driver for Vagrant is `kitchen-vagrant`

- People to work together in the same `chef-repo` and Chef server knife workflow plugin is `knife-spork`
- The preferred language for Chef is Ruby

A recipe is the collection of resources, defined using patterns such as resource names, attribute-value pairs, and actions. It is the fundamental configuration element designed to read and act in a predictable manner and authored in Ruby programming language.

A few properties are as follows:

- Include all that is required to configure the system
- To be stored in a cookbook
- For the Chef client to be used, it must be added to a run list
- It is executed in the same sequence as listed in a run list
- Chef client will run the recipe only when instructed
- Could be included in another recipe
- Might read the contents of a data bag (encrypted data bag)
- Might input the results of a search query
- Might have dependency on other recipes
- Facilitate the creation of arbitrary groupings by tagging a node
- If the recipe is constant, then there won't be any change by repeated execution

Recipe DSL is a Ruby DSL that is used to declare resources primarily from within a recipe. It also helps to ensure recipes interact with nodes (and node properties) in the expected manner. Most of the Recipe DSL methods find a specific parameter to advice Chef client on actions to take according to the node parameter.

A resource is a configuration policy statement that:

- Describes the configuration item desired state
- Declares the steps on the item required for the desired state
- Resource type is specified such as package, template, or service
- Lists additional resource properties
- Are grouped into recipes, that describe working configurations

Chef has built-in resources to cover common actions across common platforms and can be built to handle any customized situation.

With different versions of cookbooks, multiple environments of production, staging, development/testing are managed.

Cookbook template resources are used to add to recipes for dynamic generation of static text files.

To manage configuration files, **Embedded Ruby (ERB)** templates are used.

The cookbooks/templates directory contains ERB template files with Ruby expressions and statements.

The cookbooks are written consistently as per standards and tested for same.

With unit and integration testing, the cookbooks recipes are validated, testing code quality is also called syntax testing.

Test Kitchen, ChefSpec, and Foodcritic, and so on, are tools for testing Chef recipes.

The attribute files are executed in the same order as defined in the cookbook.

Chef is built on top of Ruby, it is a thin **domain-specific language (DSL)** with built-in taxonomy for customizations need of organization.

To manage environments, cookbooks, data bags, and to configure role-based access for users and groups, attributes, run lists, roles, and so on, the Chef server user interface is the Chef management console.

Chef Supermarket is the community location to share and manage. Cookbooks may be used by any Chef user or organization.

Extended Features of Chef

It is a powerful automation platform that transforms infrastructure into code that operates on the cloud, on-premises, or in a hybrid environment. Infrastructure is configured, deployed, and managed across your network irrespective of the organization size with Chef Automate. Integral parts of Chef Automate are Chef, Habitat, and InSpec.

Three open source power-packed engines are shown in the following image:

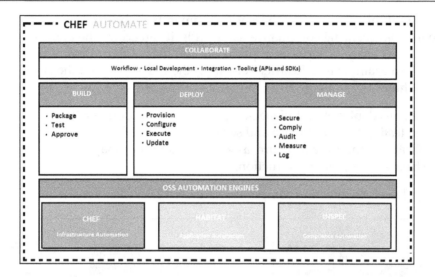

Chef is the core engine for infrastructure automation. Habitat is an application automation tool emulating concepts of containers and microservices. InSpec ensures compliance and security requirements by specifying executable code.

Habitat

Habitat comes with a prescribed packaging format for application automation; the Habitat supervisor and application dependencies are packaged and deployed as one unit. The Habitat package format defines on how to be structured, these are isolated, immutably executed for any kind of runtime environments such as a container, bare metal, or PaaS. The Habitat supervisor manages the package's peer relationships, upgrade strategy, and security policies, which are auditable as well.

InSpec

InSpec is an open source to test for adherence to security policies. It's a framework for specifying compliance, security, and policy requirements to automatically testing any node in the infrastructure. Compliance can be expressed as code and integrated into a deployment pipeline.

- InSpec using the Compliance DSL enables you to write auditing rules quickly and easily

- InSpec examines infrastructure nodes to run the tests locally or remotely

- Security, compliance, or policy issues noncompliance is logged

The InSpec audit resource framework and Chef Compliance are fully compatible.

It runs on multiple platforms with remote commands such as SSH or using Docker API, apart from ensuring compliance using APIs, it can access the database, inspect, and can restrict usage of services or protocols and the configuration of virtual machines. An example is to Restrict Telnetd or the FTP service on the client or server machines.

The continuous deployment full-stack pipeline is Chef Automate. It includes automated testing for compliance and security. The workflow provides visibility for both applications and infrastructure, as well as changes propagating throughout the pipeline from development production.

Chef High Level Architecture components are Chef DK, Chef Server, and clients:

The Chef server plays multiple roles and acts as a hub for configuration data. It stores cookbooks, applies the policies to the systems in accordance with the infrastructure, and metadata defined for each system.

Cookbook development workflow is prescribed by the Chef Development kit as below:

- Skeleton cookbook creation: A cookbook with the standard files already part of the Chef Development kit, the Berkshelf is the package manager that helps manage cookbooks and related dependencies.

- Virtual machine environment creation using Test Kitchen: Environment that develops the cookbook with the location details for performing automated testing and debugging of that cookbook during development.

- Prepare and debug the recipes for the cookbook: An iterative process to develop and test cookbooks, fix bugs, and test till they meet their purpose. Cookbooks are authored with any text editor such as Sublime Text, vim, TextMate, EditPad, and so on.

- Conduct acceptance tests: These tests are done against a full Chef server using a near production environment as opposed to development environment.

- The cookbooks that pass all the acceptance tests in the desired manner are deployed to the production environment.

Chef Automate Workflow

Chef Automate pipeline is for continuous delivery of full-stack approaches for infrastructure and applications. It facilitates safe deployment with any application, changes at high velocity, and relates infrastructure changes.

The Chef Automate pipeline quality gates are automated to move changes from a developer's workstation from deployment to production. A proposed change is approved by a team and afterwards, acceptance tests are approved and released to the respective artefact for delivery into production.

This diagram shows the workflow from development, test, and deployment of Chef code:

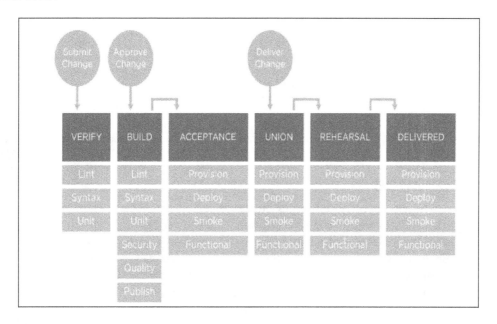

The artefact moves through the pipeline after the acceptance stage, moves to the union stage of quality assurance, rehearsal (pre-production), and delivered (production).

The Chef Automate graphical user interface provides views into operational and workflow events. Its data warehouse collects inputs from Chef, Habitat, Automate workflow, and compliance. Dashboards track each change status through the pipeline and query languages available to customize dashboards.

Compliance

Compliance issues, security risks, and outdated software can be identified by creating customizable reports with compliance rules in InSpec. There are built-in profiles with predefined rule sets for security frameworks such as **Centre for Internet Security (CIS)** benchmarks, and so on. Compliance reposting can be standalone or integrated. Also, the Chef Automate server provides high availability with fault tolerance, real-time data about your infrastructure, and consistent search results.

The Chef Compliance server facilitates centralized management of the infrastructure's compliance, performing the following tasks:

- Create and manage profiles of rules
- Test nodes as per the organization's security management life cycle regularly
- The scans are fully executed remotely; no footprint is installed on the node
- Compliance reports ensure infrastructure meets security requirements
- Auditing statistics for nodes compliance are available

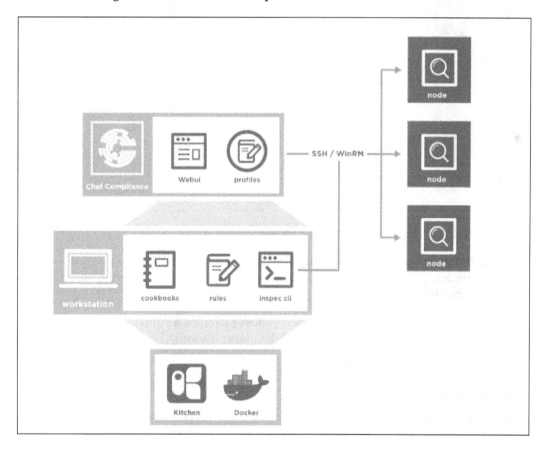

Chef compliance reports detailing multiple parameters such as node wise for patch and compliance are shown in the following:

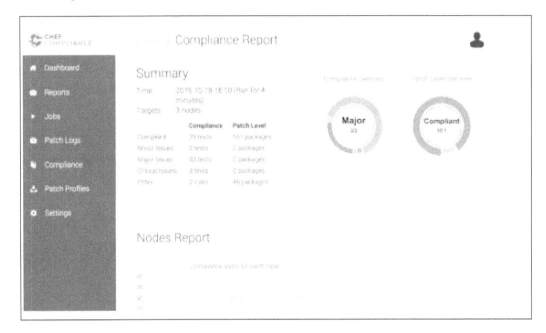

Chef Compliance Report views from Automate.

Chef Automate provides the ability to analyze compliance reports to pivot the data for either nodes, platform of the node, environment, or profiles with the ability to drill down on the information.

Chef Automate compliance control status report provides a comprehensive dashboard on major, minor, critical, patch levels, and so on.

Ansible

Ansible is a popular and powerful automation framework for continuous delivery with features and benefits are listed in the following topics:

Prominent Features

Ansible provides following features:

- Modernize
    - ° Automate existing deployment process
    - ° Manage legacy systems and process, updated like DevOps

- Migrate
    - ° Define applications once and redeploy anywhere

- DevOps
    - ° Model everything, deploy continuously

Benefits of Ansible

Using Ansible provides multiple advantages as listed following:

- Simple to use
    - ° Special coding skills not required
    - ° Tasks are executed sequentially
    - ° Get productive quickly
    - ° Automation is easily understood

- Powerful with functionality
    - ° App deployment
    - ° Configuration management
    - ° Orchestration of workflow
    - ° Orchestration of app life cycle

- Agentless
    - ° Agentless architecture
    - ° Uses OpenSSH and WinRM
    - ° No agents to exploit or update
    - ° More efficient and secure

Ansible is a multi-dimensional IT automation engine that simplifies automation of cloud provisioning, intra-service orchestration, configuration management, application deployment, and many other IT functionalities.

Ansible models your IT infrastructure by prescribing to interrelate systems for multi-tier deployments against managing the systems individually.

As discussed under features, there are neither client-side agents nor additional custom security infrastructure for Ansible. It makes deployment very simple by describing automation jobs in a plain English language called YAML and in the form of Ansible playbooks.

Ansible architecture is as shown in the following:

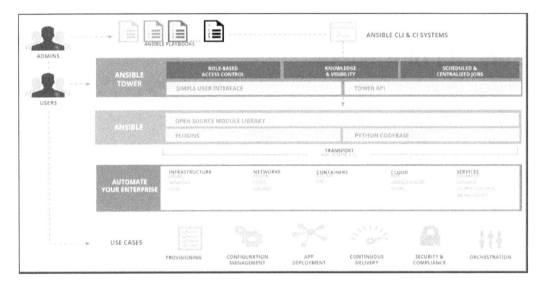

Ansible Terminology, Key Concepts, Workflow, and Usage

Ansible Tower is a web-based solution for enterprise automation frameworks designed to be the hub for controlling, securing, and managing your Ansible environment with a user interface and RESTful APIs. It provides the following rich features:

- Access control is role-based to keep the environment secure, and efficient in managing – allows sharing of SSH credentials but not transfer
- With push-button deployment access even non-privileged users can safely deploy entire applications by providing access on the fly
- Ensuring complete auditability and compliance as all Ansible automations are centrally logged
- Inventory with a wide variety of cloud sources, can be graphically managed or synced
- It's based on a robust REST API, integrates well with LDAP, and logs all jobs
- Easy integration with the continuous integration tool Jenkins, command-line tools options are available
- Supports auto scaling topologies though provisioning callback
- Ansible Tower is installed using Ansible playbooks

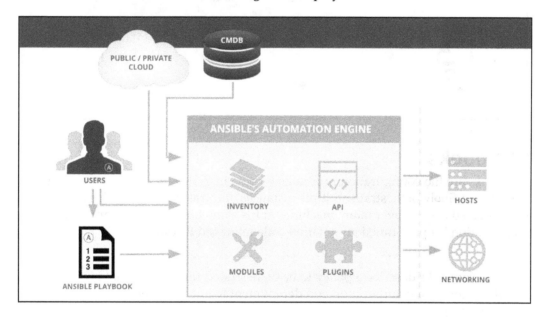

CMDB

Ansible **configuration management database (CMDB)** maintains the entire configuration information of the enterprise in the database and supports cloud creation options in multiple formats for different vendors.

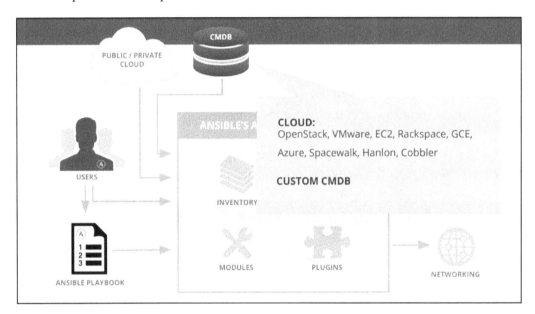

Playbooks

Playbooks are the configuration programs written in YAML to automate the systems. Ansible can finely orchestrate multiple instances of infrastructure topology with very detailed control over many machines at the same time. Ansible's approach to orchestration is finely-tuned automation code managed through simple YAML on syntax or features.

Ansible playbooks describe a policy to be orchestrated for enforcement on remote systems for configuration and deployment to enforce general IT process adherence steps.

A simple analogy is, an inventory of hosts is raw material, instruction manuals are playbooks, and Ansible modules are the tools in the workshop.

To manage configurations of deployments to remote machines, playbooks can be used at a basic level. They can sequence multi-tier rollouts involving rolling updates on a more advanced level, to interact with monitoring servers and load balancers along the way and delegate actions to other hosts.

Playbooks are developed in a basic text language conveniently designed to be human-readable. Organizing playbooks and the files can be done in multiple ways.

A simple playbook example:

```
- hosts: webservers
serial: 6 # update 6 machines at a time
roles:
- common
- webapp
- hosts: content_servers
roles:
- common
- content
```

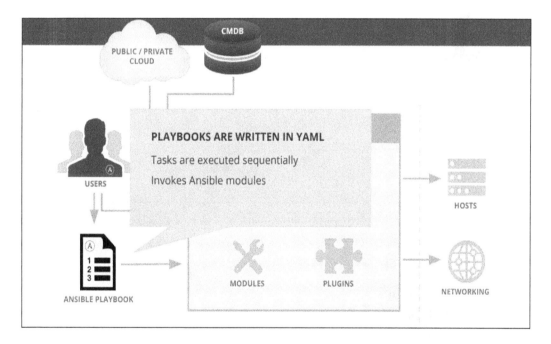

Modules

Ansible modules can control system resources, such as services, packages, or files to handle and execute system commands. These resource modules are pushed by Ansible on nodes to configure them to the desired state of the system. These Ansible modules are executed over SSH (Secured Shell) on the target nodes and removed after accomplishing the task. The module library is shipped by default with a number of modules to be executed through playbooks or directly on remote hosts. The modules can reside on any machine, there is no concept of servers, daemons, or databases to maintain them. The modules and libraries are customizable, typically created with any terminal program, a text editor, and to keep track of changes to the content, the version control system is used effectively.

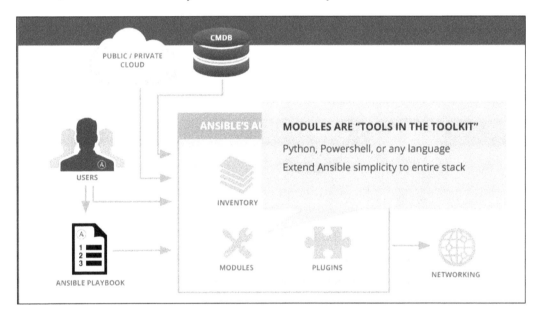

Inventory

Ansible inventory is a list of resources:

- Hosts and groups
- Host variables
- Group variables
- Groups of groups and group variables
- Default groups
- Splitting out group and host and specific data

- List of inventory behavioral Parameters
- Non-SSH connection types

Ansible, through the inventory list, works on multiple systems in the infrastructure simultaneously. The dynamic inventory mechanism allows multiple inventory files to be flexible and customizable at the same time through inventory plugins. The inventory list can be in a default location or specify inventory file location of your choice from dynamic or cloud sources, EC2, Rackspace, OpenStack, or different formats.

Here's what a plain text inventory file looks like:

```
[webservers]
www1.example.com
www2.example.com
[dbservers]
db0.example.com
db1.example.com
```

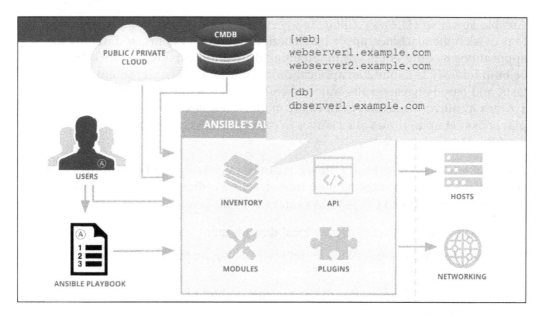

Plugins

Ansible's core functionality is augmented by a number of handy plugins and can be customized in JSON (Ruby, Python, Bash, and so on). Plugins can connect to any data source, extend the connection types for transport other than with SSH, call back for logs, and even add new server-side behaviors.

Ansible Tower

Offers multiple features such as:

- LDAP, AD, SAML, and other directories can be connected
- Access control engines that are role based
- Credentials without exposure storage
- Simple for first time users
- Smart Search enabled information lookup
- Configure automation at runtime
- REST API based integration with processes and tools
- Tower clusters to extend capacity

Ansible Tower can invoke multi-playbook workflows to link any number of playbooks, with different inventories, run as different users, run as batch, or with different credentials.

Ansible Tower workflows facilitate many complex operations, build workflows to provision the machines, apply base configurations of systems, and deploy the applications by different teams maintaining different playbooks. A workflow can be built for CI/CD to build an application, deploy to a test environment, run tests, and based on test results, automatically promotes the application. Ansible Tower's intuitive workflow editor easily models complex processes with different playbooks set up to run as alternatives in case of success or failure of a prior workflow playbook.

A typical workflow may be as follows, it can be effectively used on multiple systems quickly without taking their infrastructure offline. To achieve continuous deployment, automated QA is vital to mature to this level:

- Script automation to deploy local development VMs
- CI system such as Jenkins to deploy to a staging environment on every code change
- The deploy job executes the test scripts on build for pass/fail for every deploy
- Upon success of the deploy job, the same playbook is run against production inventory

The Ansible Tower workflow brings the following features and functionality:

- Jobs schedule
- Built-in notifications to inform the teams
- Stabilized API to connect to existing tooling and processes
- New workflows to model entire processes

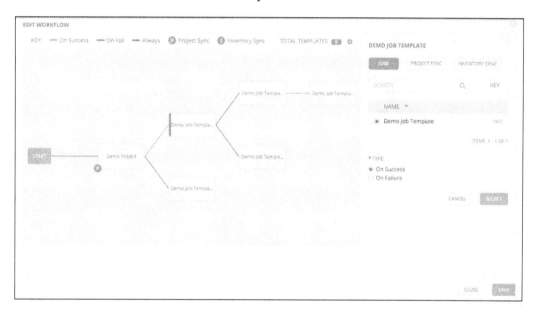

The Ansible Tower dashboard (refer to the image) offers functionality as listed:

- Dashboard and real-time automation updates
- Graphical inventory management
- Integrated RBAC with credential management

Ansible Vault

Ansible Vault is a feature to keep sensitive data in encrypted form, for example passwords or keys as opposed to saving them as plain text in roles or playbooks. These vault files can be placed in source control or distributed to multiple locations. The data files such as Ansible tasks, handlers, arbitrary files, even binary files can be encrypted with Vault as well. These are decrypted at the destination on target host.

Ansible Galaxy

Ansible Galaxy is an open source website designed for community information and contributing to collaborate on building IT automation solutions to bring together administrators and developers. There are preconfigured roles to download and jump start automation projects with Galaxy search index. These are also available with a GitHub account.

Testing Strategies with Ansible

Though testing is a very organizational and site-specific concept, Ansible Integrated Testing with Ansible playbooks is designed as an ordered and fail-fast system. It facilitates embed testing directly in Ansible playbooks through a push-based mechanism.

Ansible playbooks are models of desired-state of the system that will ensure the things declared, such as services to be started and packages installed, are in accordance with declarative statements. Ansible is an order-based system on unhandled errors. A host will fail immediately and prevent further configuration of that host and shows them as a summary at the end of the Ansible run. Ansible is a multi-tier orchestration system to incorporate tests into the playbook run, either as tasks or roles.

Testing the application for integrating tests of infrastructure before deployment in the workflow will be effective to check the code quality and performance before it moves to production systems. Being push-based, the checks and balances in the workflow and even upgrading is very easy to maintain on the localhost or test servers.

Monitoring

Enterprise monitoring is a primary activity and it categorizes monitoring development milestones, application logs, server health, operations, infrastructure, vulnerabilities, deployments, and user activity. These are accomplished with:

- Collecting and key messages
- Mature monitoring tools
- Avoid perceptions and making decisions based on uncertainty
- Participative monitoring and evaluation

- Selecting and using right indicators
- Interpreting indicator results in business context
- Real-time data collection
- Managing data and information

Development Milestones: Monitoring of development milestones is an indicator of how well your DevOps adoption strategy is working by gaining insights of the actual process and team effectively. Some of the metrics are sprint scope changes, bugs count of field and fixed, and the ratio of promised-to-delivered features. These metrics are the drivers on team effectiveness and adherence to the schedule, this monitoring is built-in as an Agile plugin for issue tracking.

Code Vulnerabilities: Monitoring vulnerabilities in application code, lists the weaknesses induced in the top-level code by insecure coding practices. These can be addressed by conducting regular code reviews or changing third-party dependencies, and so on.

Deployments: Deployment monitoring is configuring your build servers to have some monitoring built into the process to notify the team. Notification-capable continuous integration servers communicate with chat servers and promptly alert teams of failed builds and deployments.

Application log output: Application log output to be planned for centralized logging if services are distributed to gain full benefit, errors and exceptions provides value in real-time. The ability to trace notifications from error-producing code in a searchable format generates benefit, before production move.

Server Health: Monitoring of uptime and performance of available resources downed or over-utilized servers fall in this category. Intrusion detection and health monitoring systems being on the same notification pipeline will provide additional value.

Activity Monitoring: User activity monitoring is both feature development and the scaling of infrastructure. Along with monitoring development milestones volume of data is monitored.

The centralized storage of consolidated logging data for application logs, user activity monitoring, and project history enhances the value to detect and analyze in a global context correlating different log sources about the state of the application and the project.

Splunk

Splunk is a popular application monitoring tool to gain real-time visibility into DevOps-driven application delivery for Continuous Delivery or Continuous Integration to move from concept to production quickly. Splunk enterprise helps improve the business impact of application delivery by enhancing velocity and quality.

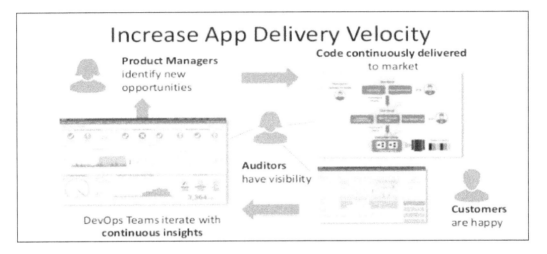

Splunk improves code quality with the following benefits:

- Resolve code issues before customers see them
- Detect and fix issues related to production faster
- Objective metrics are available to ensure code is operational and meets quality SLAs

Splunk is a platform to capture and record all the activity and behavior of your customers, machine data, users, transactions, applications, servers, networks, and mobile devices.

The Splunk platform enhances its business impact by integrated real-time insights from application development to testing to production monitoring. It provides cohesive views across all stages of the delivery life cycle as opposed to discrete release components.

Real-time visibility into business-relevant data for business and DevOps leaders on both development and operations, such as application performance, usage, revenue systems, cart fulfillment, and registration data provides insights to better plan inventory and report and improve the customer experience.

Development life cycle integration and visibility across diverse, multiple supported phases and applications is supported:

Operations lifecycle integration and visibility across diverse, multiple supported phases and application is supported. Applications are delivered faster using analytics:

- End-to-end visibility across every DevOps delivery tool chain component
- Correlated insights that iterate faster across the application delivery lifecycle
- Measuring and benchmarking release contributions and improving DevOps team efficiency

Splunk helps organizations by enabling a feedback loop to business leaders, evaluating the real impact of code changes on their customers. Continuous interaction helps to build more intelligence about machine behavior and deep asset models.

The benefits reflect the business impact of application delivery:

- Gain new business insights by correlating business metrics with code changes
- Enhance user experience through delivery of better-performing code
- Delivering more secure and compliant code improves reputation

Nagios Monitoring Tool for Infrastructure

There are multiple variants of the Nagios open source tool for monitoring mission-critical infrastructure components specific to each segment on any operating system:

- Network monitoring software
- Network traffic monitoring
- Server (Linux, Windows) monitoring
- Application monitoring tools
- Web application monitoring
- Monitoring core engine and a basic web interface
- Nagios core plugins package with add-ons
- Nagios log server security threats with audit system

Nagios facilitates monitoring of the network for problems such as overloaded data links, network connections, monitoring routers, switches, problems caused by overloaded of crashed servers, and so on.

Nagios can deliver the metric results in a variety of visual representations and reports to monitor availability, uptime, and response time of every node on the network with both agent-based and agent-less monitoring.

Effective application monitoring with Nagios enables organizations to quickly detect applications, services, or process problems, and take corrective action to prevent downtime for your application users.

Nagios tools for monitoring of applications and application state extends to Windows applications, Linux applications, Unix applications, and web applications. It has an active community collaboration network.

The router monitoring capabilities offer benefits such as immediate notification on unresponsive machines, early warning by detecting network outages and protocol failures, increased servers, services, and application availability.

Windows monitoring with Nagios enables increased servers, services, and application availability, quick detection of network outages, failed services, processes, batch jobs and protocol failures, and so on. The extensive metrics are gathered for system metrics, event logs, applications (IIS, Exchange, and so on), services (Active Directory, DHCP, service states, process states, performance counters, and so on).

Nagios – Enterprise Server and Network Monitoring Software

Built-in advanced features are:

- Integrated overview of sources, checks, network flow data, and so on, provided with comprehensive dashboard
- Alert of suspicious network activity by security and reliability network analyzer.
- Insights and drill down options on network traffic, bandwidth, overall network health, and so on, with advanced visualizations
- Monitor network usage of specific applications, custom application monitoring, custom queries, views, and reports are available
- Historical network flow data with subsets of network flow information through specialized views
- Abnormal activity alerts with automated alert system example bandwidth usage exceeds specified thresholds

- Integrated metrics of network analyzer server loads with hard disk space availability

Integrated Dashboards for Network Analysis, Monitoring, and Bandwidth

The Nagios dashboard with multiple monitoring options such as source groups, Server CPU, disk usage, and so on, can be extended and customized with many more choices based on business requirements.

Summary

In this lesson, we learned infrastructure configuration management as code for continuous deployment with tools such as Chef, Puppet, and Ansible and also continuous monitoring process with tools Splunk and Nagios.

With this, we've come to the end of this book. I hope you'd a smooth journey and gained a lot of knowledge on DevOps.

I wish you all the best for your future projects. Keep learning and exploring!

Assessments

1. Which among the following is the order for continuous delivery alignment?

    1. Build, Code, Integrate, Release
    2. Code, Build, Integrate, Release
    3. Build, Code, Release, Integrate
    4. Code, Build, Release, Integrate

2. Which among the following are tools for continuous deployment?

    1. Git
    2. Nagios
    3. JUnit
    4. Jenkins

3. A resource is a configuration policy statement that:
    1. Includes all that is required to configure the system
    2. Facilitates the creation of arbitrary groupings by tagging a node
    3. Describes the desired state of the configured item
    4. Executes in the same sequence as listed in a run list

4. Which of the following comes with a prescribed packaging format for application automation.
    1. Habitat
    2. InSpec
    3. Chef
    4. Ansible

5. _____ are the configuration programs written in YAML to automate the systems.
    1. CMDB
    2. Modules
    3. Playbooks
    4. Inventory

Assessment Answers

Lesson 1: Introduction to DevOps

Question Number	Answer
1	3
2	1
3	2
4	4
5	1

Lesson 2: DevOps Framework

Question Number	Answer
1	1
2	3
3	2
4	3
5	1

Lesson 3: DevOps - Continuous Integration and Delivery

Question Number	Answer
1	3
2	False
3	4
4	2
5	4

Lesson 4: DevOps Continuous Deployment

Question Number	Answer
1	2
2	4
3	3
4	1
5	3